Praise for *They Call Me "Mr. De"*

"In *They Call Me 'Mr. De,'* Frank DeAngelis reflects on the enduring resilience and hope of the Columbine community that grieved and healed together in the aftermath of that terrible day in April of 1999. This book is a testament to the power of compassion in the face of crisis and the age-old belief that leaders are not born but made."

—President Bill Clinton

"Frank DeAngelis offers us a rare window into a personal journey few have traveled and fewer have paved. Through his candor about helping a community recover from an unspeakable tragedy and his unwavering focus on relationships, he shows us how respect for others, empathetic leadership, and bravery can improve the world and deepen our humanity."

—Kristina Anderson, founder, The Koshka Foundation
for Safe Schools

"An incredible book written by an incredible human being. For some reason, Frank DeAngelis was put in the position to lead a community through one of the worst school tragedies in history. *They Call Me 'Mr. De'* illustrates Frank's leadership, compassion, faith, and vulnerability at a time when those around Frank needed him most. It is an honor to know this great man and call him my friend."

—Scott Bemis, retired president and
publisher *Denver Business Journal*

"Frank DeAngelis sounds a clarion call of hope in a time that, if we're not careful, can seem hopeless—especially to our youngest generations. Tempered in the crucible of unimaginable tragedy, DeAngelis' voice emerges optimistic and inspiring. Please read this book. We need its message now more than ever."

—Steve Farber, author, *The Radical Leap, The Radical Edge,* and
Greater Than Yourself; founder and chairman,
The Extreme Leadership Institute

"While the world was watching, Frank DeAngelis worked a miracle by allowing his humanity to be his standard! This book is for every leader in every profession; it is the truth about trauma, recovery, and moving forward while never forgetting."

—**J. Kevin Cameron**, executive director, North American Center for Threat Assessment and Trauma Response

"Surely the best, most personal, profound, emotional, heart-wrenching, compelling book ever written about the senseless and tragic attack at Columbine. Irrefutable proof that we *must*, *can* and *are* doing more to ensure safe schools. Frank DeAngelis has given us the gift of honesty, resilience, and recovery. Now it's up to us. No amount of theory from those who have never experienced a school shooting can replace the truth and power of experience of our hero Frank DeAngelis. *They Call Me 'Mr. De'* should be required reading for every educator, school resource officer, and parent."

—**Theresa Campbell**, president, Safer Schools Together

"There was a realization on April 20, 1999, that our nation was catapulted into an entirely new world of school safety. Both heartwarming and heartbreaking, *They Call Me 'Mr. De,'* encapsulates the fervor of the time and propels us into the present moment as the world of school safety is shifting once again. Frank DeAngelis encourages us to focus on one of the most important and often overlooked concepts of school safety: building relationships with students, parents, and school staff. His recommendations, derived from his experience on that fateful day, are crucial to furthering our national mission to keep every school and student safe."

—**Mo Canady**, executive director, National Association of School Resource Officers

"The book is a true and unique testimony on the Columbine tragedy and its aftermath, and an insight into the great heart and spirit of one of its heroes, Columbine Principal Frank DeAngelis. DeAngelis has been a blessing for his students, community and our nation before, during, and after the Columbine shooting."

—**Jon DeStefano**, president, Jefferson County School Board (1999)

"This book is about family and faith. Frank led Columbine as his precious family. His faith and those around him gave him strength which he used to help mend broken hearts. The world is better when we believe we are part of the family."

—**Ron Castagna**, principal, Lakewood High School (1996-2014)

"Frank came to my attention the first hour of the shooting, when a sophomore in her gym uniform told a harrowing story of escaping gunfire in the hallway. When I asked if she was afraid, said, 'No, because the principal was with me.' *Really?* All afternoon and all that week, I heard similar depictions of a principal unlike any I'd ever met. Covering the Columbine kids was heartbreaking. They were the first to face such a horror, and recovery was uncharted territory. No one knew what it would take to get them to the other side of this emotional wasteland. They needed someone exceptional. They already had him."

—**Dave Cullen**, magazine contributor and author of *Columbine* and *Parkland*

"This book is a chilling, realistic account of the trials and tribulations of a man who is larger than life. Frank, a true national treasure, has been the guiding light for so many others who have experienced tragedy. Learning from the tragic events on April 20, 1999, Frank took those lessons and continues to tirelessly help a nation prepare. He is a true inspiration and I'm honored to call him a friend."

—**Deputy Chief AJ DeAndrea**, Arvada Police Department

"Frank's story is perhaps the most undertold story of the Columbine shootings. This book is compelling and riveting. Even though I was the principal at the high school near Columbine during the weeks and months that followed, I learned so much more reading this book. In an era when we search for heroes, or perhaps angels among us, Frank easily qualifies for both titles. What an amazing person he is. There are, perhaps, a handful of people in the world who could have brought about the healing to the Columbine community. If there was the equivalent to the Medal of Honor for educators, Frank should be the first recipient. His story, contained in this book is powerful and uplifting."

—**Jim Ellis**, principal (Bell Middle School, Chatfield High School, Ralston Valley High School)

"Those of us lucky enough to call Frank DeAngelis friend, family, teacher, mentor, coach, boss, or 'Mr. De,' draw great inspiration from the stories of his beloved Columbine, the staff he considers family, the students that will always be 'his kids,' and the faith, family, and friends that supported him through it all. An unwavering servant leader, Frank has given greatly to many. Here he shares more—deeply and honestly—so that we too might *never forget.*"

—Michele Gay, mother of Josephine Gay and co-founder
and executive director, Safe and Sound Schools

"The best book I have read about the Columbine High School shootings. Every once in a while, in our lives we get to meet a great person. Frank DeAngelis is one of those."

—Monsignor Ken Leone, Denver, Colorado

"This is a book about a faith journey. A journey not only for Mr. De but of everyone. A work that reminds us that we are never alone that we are on this journey together the good times and the tragedies. I can remember where I was on that tragic day as can most people, but I couldn't imagine the events that followed after the cameras left. Mr. De, in this book, tells the story of the aftermath. I know Mr. De as a man of faith, a leader who doesn't check out when the bell rings at the end of the day. Mr. De gives me hope and I am blessed to call him a friend."

—Fr. Sean McGrath, former pastor,
St. Frances Cabrini Church,
Littleton, Colorado

"Reading *They Call Me 'Mr. De'* is a truly literary experience, one that transports the reader to a chair across from Frank DeAngelis as he shares the story of his life. Interwoven with stories from those that know him best, this memoir captures the authenticity, strength, resilience, faith, and hope of a man who faced one of the worst tragedies in U.S. history and not only came out on top but also brought his community with him. For anyone who wants to understand the true meaning of Columbine and its spirit, this book is a must-read."

—Dr. Jaclyn Schildkraut, associate professor
of Public Justice, SUNY Oswego

"In this book, Frank DeAngelis tells a story that only he can tell. He shares a little bit about growing up in North Denver, but truly his life has been defined by his professional commitment to and his love for Columbine High School and its community. On April 20, 1999, Frank's life was changed forever when that tragic senseless event occurred.

"'Mr. De' is revered in the Columbine community, our school district, and the nation because he had the courage, skill and heart to lead his beloved school community through uncharted waters in the aftermath of this horrific tragedy. He followed that, with time as his ally, by leading the school and community to the light of recovery and hope. This was a journey that no one ever plans or hopes to take.

"Once I started this book, I could not put it down, and I could not keep my eyes dry. Thank you, Frank DeAngelis, for having the courage to accurately share this complex journey with all of us. Your leadership, values, and love made this story possible, and it documents a classic triumph of the human spirit over the forces of evil. Anyone who has ever stepped foot into a school building can benefit from this compelling story."

—**Ron Mitchell**, past Columbine High School principal, Jefferson County School Board president, and friend

"There are lies. There are rumors. There are myths about the events of April 20th, 1999, at Columbine High School. Lies, rumors, and myths that are shaping generations. There is also a personal story. A transparent story from a man who not only survived the day, but defined the aftermath. This is that story.

"Frank DeAngelis, 'Mr. De', shares his experiences before, during and after the killings at Columbine. Some of the read isn't easy. It's a tough conversation. But it's also joyous and wise and strong. This book is peppered with life lessons that everyone should see.

"It is also a story of friendships: friendships forged in the aftermath of tragedy, unlikely friendships that would never have occurred without a loss—friendships that are gifts. You might even call it a club. Thank you Frank for sharing your journey."

—**John-Michael Keyes and Ellen Stoddard-Keyes**, founders of The I Love U Guys Foundation

"I found Frank's personal story to be a very powerful journey starting from his early years growing up Italian in the Denver Metro Area and finally arriving at Columbine High School. He uses stories and experiences to give the reader an inside and close view of life in a normal suburban high school. However, in Chapter 5, his journey transcends into the darkness and tragedy of April 20, 1999.

"Frank's descriptions of the beginning events, the responses, and the recovery make the readers feel like they are in the center of the storm. These chapters were very impactful for me personally since I was one of the many responders on scene and was involved with the recovery process. His stories and writing style allows the reader to empathize with those impacted that day and identify with the psychological footprint left by the tragedy.

"Frank's journey then takes the readers into a place people never want to venture, that of a new normal due to bad events. The book ties everything together in the final chapters as it prompts the readers to face up to the realities and challenges in dealing with our new normal. His final chapter provides a touching close to those who lost their lives and the family members whose lives were changed forever. Frank, thank you for sharing your story with us."

—**John Nicoletti**, PhD, ABPP board certified specialist in
police and public safety psychology

"Frank DeAngelis' leadership is inspiring, and his insights and compassion are balm on the wounds of communities wracked by gun violence and other tragedies. At this pivotal moment in our nation, *They Call Me 'Mr. De,'* is a must-read for all who seek a pathway to healing and believe that pain should not be wasted, since it can be a source of hope and redemption."

—**Gerda Weissmann Klein**, Holocaust survivor
and founder of Citizenship Counts,
recipient of the Presidential Medal of Freedom

"Frank DeAngelis is a man of courage. His book is truly a reflection of bravery and compassion. During the Columbine tragedy, Frank modeled leadership in the finest sense. His words in this book portray both the heartbreak and the triumph of leadership in the most difficult of times. I worked with Frank through the Columbine tragedy. I can attest that he has much to teach all of us about strength and commitment. I can attest that he was a beacon of light in darkness. I can attest that the school, his colleagues, and the community will be forever grateful for his leadership. As you read this book, I hope that it touches your heart and your intellect. I hope you find the story as tragic and as uplifting as I did. I am eternally grateful that Frank has now told the story. Although Frank would dispute some of these descriptors, he is a friend, a colleague, and a hero."

—**Dr. Cynthia Stevenson,** senior instructor at University of Colorado at Denver, and former superintendent of Jefferson County School District

"Frank DeAngelis' story is a journey of recovery, healing, and transformation. There are forward steps and mis-steps, faith questioned and affirmed, love lost and found, and the search for peace in the aftermath of the unspeakable horror of mass murder. And it is a journey that continues to this day."

—**Mark Wolf**, Columbine High School parent, Columbine High School basketball coach

They Call Me "Mr. De"

The Story of Columbine's Heart, Resilience, and Recovery

Frank DeAngelis
Former Principal of Columbine High School

They Call Me "Mr. De"
© 2019 by Frank DeAngelis

This book is available at special discounts when purchased in quantity for use as premiums, promotions, fundraisers, or for educational use. For inquiries and details, contact the publisher at books@daveburgessconsulting.com.

Published by Dave Burgess Consulting, Inc.
San Diego, CA
DaveBurgessConsulting.com

Cover Design by Genesis Kohler
Cover Photo and Author photo by John Leyba
Editing and Interior Design by My Writers' Connection

Library of Congress Control Number: 2018965585
Hardback ISBN: 978-1-949595-06-2
Paperback ISBN: 978-1-949595-05-5
Ebook ISBN: 978-1-949595-07-9

First Printing: March 2019

Dedication

In Loving Memory of . . .

Cassie Bernall

Steven Curnow

Corey DePooter

Kelly Fleming

Matthew Kechter

Daniel Mauser

Daniel Rohrbough

Dave Sanders

Rachel Scott

Isaiah Shoels

John Tomlin

Lauren Townsend

Kyle Velasquez

To the staff members of Columbine High School
in the 1998–99 school year.
We always will have a special bond:

Claudia Abbott	Alan DiGiosio	Ken Holden
Lee Andres	Michelle DiManna	Peter Horvath
Leland Andres	Peggy Dodd	Sondra Inman
Tony Arnold	Mariel Fankhouser	Joyce Jankowski
Judy Asbury	Jan Fiedler	Doug Johnson
Bob Asleson	Dan Fleener	Tom Johnson
Rick Bath	Laura Freund	Alan Jungerman
Catherine Baumgartner	Eric Friesen	Kim Karamigios
Candace Birch-Sterling	Kent Friesen	Lois Kean
Bill Biskup	Kathy Frommer	Liz Keating
Jud Blatchford	Jay Gallentine	Syd Keating
Lisa Bohack	Rebecca Gomez-Bailey	Judy Kelly
Cathy Bonin	Judy Greco	Charlotte Killion
Brandon Brookfield	Carolyn Green	Eric Kritzer
Jane Brug	Brenda Haggard	Kevin Land
Ray Bundy	Terry Havens	Leslie Layman
Amy Burnett	Ellin Hayes	Julie Lebsack
Brad Butts	Gordon Hayes	Kiki Leyba
Anna Cabrera	Gretchen Hazelwood	Sue Liane
Tim Capra	William Hebner	Rich Long
Sue Caruthers	Laverne Helm	Andy Lowry
Ryan Collins	Josh Herold	Cheryl Lucas
Doug Craft	Kathy Herring	Cathy Lutz
Al Cram	Shirley Hickman	Kris MacCauley
Joe Cunningham	Joe Higgins	Mona Madden
Jon Curtis	Barb Hirokawa	Susan Madory
Suzanne Dewlaney	Cindy Hoffman	Becke Mandel

Troy Manuello

Joe Marshall

Rudy Martin

Andrew Marton

Lori McMullen

Lisa McWilliams

Steve Meier

Darlene Mesch

Marilou Metcalf

Chris Mikesell

Theresa Miller

Alma Moore

Ivory Moore

Sharon Morrissey

Cheryl Mosier

Chris Mosier

Kate Moulton

Samantha Myers

Marlene Nederman

Karen Nielsen

Patti Nielson

Tommie Nykanen

Robin Ortiz

Ron Osendorf

Monette Park

Susan Peters

Frank Petersen

Shirley Pierce

Craig Place

Jackie Reardon

Chris Redmerski

Paula Reed

Nolene Regnier

Maria Reschke

Randon Rodarte

Tammy Rumer

Carol Samson

Dave Sanders

Linda Sands

Joe Savino

Libby Scheneider

Penny Schroeder

Dave Smith

Gina Stallsworth

Patti Stevens

Bruce Stoeklen

Karen Studenka

Mary Swanson

Gary Talloco

Shawn Tank

Barb Thoms

Linda Tibijas

Tom Tonelli

Kevin Tucker

Pua Warnke

Lisa Wasiefcko

Jason Webb

Carole Weld

Susan White

Dick Will

Bev Williams

Capri Wyatt

Patti Zawadski

Penny Zerr

To the other staff members and to students
of Columbine High School, past, present,
and future, I appreciate you.

Contents

Foreword
by Tommy Spaulding

When the world hears these three words—Columbine High School—unfortunately, most think about two other words: school shooting. We will never forget the horrific events that took place at Columbine High School on April 20, 1999. We will never forget the twelve students and one teacher who were killed. And we will never forget all those who were tragically affected on that day. But the Columbine story is more than just one day. There is a beautiful side to the story. The story of one man who gave his life to those three words: Columbine High School. The story of a high school principal who transformed the legacy of Columbine with one word—*love*.

I had the honor of writing about my dear friend, Frank DeAngelis, in my last book, *The Heart-Led Leader*. When you ask a parent how many kids they have, most respond by saying one, two, three, etc. When you ask Frank DeAngelis how many kids he has, his response says it all. *Thousands*.

I've visited Columbine High School many times to see my friend Frank speak to his students. And I'll tell you, I've never been inside a public high school like Columbine, where you can smell, feel, and taste acceptance and grace in every corner of the building. Walking the halls between classes with Frank was an experience unlike any I've ever had. Students continually call out, "Hey Mr. De!" "Hey Coach De!" "Hey Papa De!" Frank knew almost everyone by name. He gave hugs, knuckles, and high fives. He encouraged them. He breathed love into each and every student and teacher. In the fifteen years between the tragedy and his retirement, Frank helped transform the site of one of America's darkest moments into a beacon of light, hope, and promise. And most of all, a beacon of love.

Every morning, for years, I've received a text message from Frank. He sends me a Bible verse, a quote, or words of affirmation. And then he tells me three beautiful words: I love you. Every time. I joke with my wife, Jill, that Frank tells me he loves me more than she does! There is not a person in the world that I text every day. Tell them I love them *every* day. But Frank does.

If I had to list the five most influential men in my life who have helped shaped who I've become, Frank DeAngelis would be on that list. But the thing is, thousands of former students, teachers, and parents would also say the same. We have a lot to learn from this great man. And the pages that follow are a roadmap that can transform your family, your company, your organization, and your community with Frank's secret Italian sauce—*love*.

Introduction

The Last Commencement

I was the principal at Colorado's Columbine High School on April 20, 1999.

I remained principal for fifteen more years.

Virtually every day at the school, I heard variations of *How can you do this? How can you go back? How can you walk those same halls? How can you stand to be reminded every day?*

Many friends and colleagues urged me to move on. I refused to seek or accept a transfer to another school in Jefferson County or move to the Jeffco Public Schools central administration. I needed to be at Columbine. I wanted to be there; I couldn't walk away. Not from the kids, not from the high school, and not from the suburban school community to the southwest of downtown Denver. I wanted to see to it that Columbine came to define something other than tragedy. I wanted it to become a story of courage, love, heart, resilience, and recovery. I wanted to lead the way to that healing.

In the spring of 2014, I looked out from the stage at Fiddler's Green Amphitheatre in Greenwood Village at the more than four hundred Columbine seniors. They would be my last class. I had been at the school for thirty-five years. Before becoming principal in 1996 and spending eighteen school years in that job, I had served seventeen years in a number of roles, including a social studies teacher, dean of students, assistant principal, and coach.

These kids knew me, and always would know me, as "Mr. De." Well, that or "Coach De" or "Papa De."

They were *my* kids.

That day, after taking a selfie with my final graduating class behind me (proving that you *can* teach a veteran educator new tricks), emotion choked my voice as I spoke to those seniors:

"My first class was the class of '97, and my last is this class," I said. "We are family. We are Columbine. Once a Rebel, always a Rebel. You've made me a proud papa. I love you."

Teacher and coach Ivory Moore then went through an emotion-filled school tradition, leading us in our school chant: "We Are . . . Columbine." It built to a crescendo and illustrated that sometimes simple is the most effective approach.

Looking out on those fresh faces, students filled with dreams of what might be for them, I thought back to the promise I made at the vigil held on April 21, 1999, at Light of the World Catholic Church. That tearful morning, with school district officials and politicians listening, I vowed to the students I would remain principal until the classes enrolled at Columbine at the time of the tragedy had graduated.

That would have taken me through the Class of 2002.

Soon, though, I extended that to cover the kids attending classes in the Columbine feeder system in April 1999 as well. That committed me through the Class of 2012.

I reached 2012 on the job . . . and kept going.

I stayed on, at least in part, because a parent informed me her child was in the first year of a two-year preschool program in April 1999 and wouldn't graduate until 2013. Those kids, as young as they were in 1999, were mine too. So I stayed through the 2013 commencement and went one more year. Suddenly, or so it seemed, spring of 2014 arrived. I knew it would be my final graduation ceremony as principal of Columbine High School. I was finishing up.

Most of those kids in front of me at Fiddler's Green, the Class of 2014, had been three years old on April 20, 1999. They knew my history, knew my commitment, and knew I loved them and that I wasn't hesitant about showing it.

As a school and as a community, we had been through so much. Outsiders wanted to fixate on the horrors or on the killers, but we remembered the dead and wounded. We honored them by turning "Columbine" into that story of heart, love, resilience, courage, and recovery. Every day I reminded myself, our students, staff members, and anyone else who would listen, "We were a great school, we *are* a great school, and we will continue to be a great school. The members of the Columbine community make it great." At the one-year anniversary of the tragedy, we coined the phrase, "A Time to Remember, a Time to Hope." Those words, along with "Never Forget," are still appropriate and often cited.

The students crossed the stage to receive their diplomas from the dignitaries and then found me waiting at the bottom of the steps to congratulate them. The hugs were plentiful, and I knew we had succeeded in transforming the story. Together we made it through the heartache, anger, and despair.

That is the true and important Columbine story nearly twenty years after the murders.

Since retiring in 2014, I've been telling the story to audiences across the United States, Canada, and Europe. I've spoken to leaders in business and education, to mental health groups, to judges, prosecutors, and justices, to district attorneys, to firefighters, police officers, and other first responders, and to students at school assemblies and leadership academies. Thousands have heard me speak about the Columbine story, and thousands more will hear it in the foreseeable future.

At my presentations, I usually am asked if I am writing a book or told I *should* write one.

Finally, here it is. It's time.

In the days and years after the killings, I had to be guarded in my responses and public comments about the two murderers and the events of the day. I couldn't aggressively respond to the media's misstatements and exaggerations or the internet-driven myths. Lawsuits were pending against the school district and Jefferson County, and I was named in eight of them. I was ordered not to address issues tied to the litigation. Even if that hadn't been the case, I wanted to keep the focus on the recovery while respecting the memories and the families of murdered students: Cassie Bernall, Steven Curnow, Corey DePooter, Kelly Fleming, Matthew Kechter, Daniel Mauser, Daniel Rohrbough, Rachel Scott, Isaiah Shoels, John Tomlin, Lauren Townsend, and Kyle Velasquez.

I wanted to honor my dear friend, teacher-coach Dave Sanders, who was murdered that day.

I wanted to support the twenty-six others who were physically injured or wounded—and the countless others in our school and community whose hearts were forever scarred by what we'd witnessed.

On the personal level, the horrific events of April 20, 1999, don't define me as much as does the strength of the Columbine student body, staff members, and community. I'm confident that my love for young people and my job resonates with those who have made public education their careers. I needed Columbine—its people, its heart—more than it needed me.

During my presentations, I tell audiences of my background, how I turned to education and coaching after realizing the New

York Yankees weren't going to draft and sign me, and that my back-up plan of accounting wasn't for me. I tell them how I handled the tragedy, not just that day, but for years beyond. People in those audiences feel a sense of empathy; a bond of sorts forms as they come to understand how we fought and transformed the story—how we did it *together*.

This book includes input from my siblings, Anthony DeAngelis and LuAnn DeAngelis Dwyer; my high school sweetheart and wife, Diane (there's a story there, and we'll get to it in a bit); my life-long best friend, Rick DeBell; my high school teacher, baseball coach and mentor Chris Dittman; and, finally, my Columbine compatriots, Tom Tonelli and Kiki Leyba, both terrific teachers who, as of this writing, still are on the school faculty. Tom is a 1988 Columbine graduate who joined the faculty in 1994. Kiki dropped out of high school at age sixteen and earned his GED while working in construction. He attended Metropolitan State in Denver, did his student teaching at Columbine, then began his teaching career with us in 1998–99. My motivation in including their voices is to add to the portrait and narrative of our story and not to be showered with praise, with Kiki and Tom as representative voices of the Columbine constituency. Ricky, by the way, good-naturedly held out for a payment of $3.82, seeking to match the combined prices of a cannoli, Tuddy Toots, Little Devil, and a Coke at Carbone's in the North Denver of our youth!

Chapter One

Where Have You Gone, Joe DiMaggio?

I grew up in a large, Italian-American Catholic family where faith, family, and friends meant everything. North Denver's Our Lady of Mount Carmel Church was the center of our world.

My dad's name was Louis, but nobody called him that except maybe our priest. He was "Sonny." Raised in Bloomfield, New Jersey, he and my uncle Vito were stationed at Lowry Air Force Base during the Korean War, and both met and fell in love with Denver-area girls. My mom, Evelyn, grew up in the Welby area on the north side of the metro area, and my aunt, Florence, was from North Denver. The area, roughly a mile north of Denver's Mile High Stadium and to the west of downtown, was the gathering point for Italian immigrants who found work at the railroad or in other endeavors.

My folks, who are still living, were married at Mount Carmel in 1953. They lived in New Jersey for about six months after their marriage, then returned to Denver for good, at first moving into the other half of a duplex owned by my mom's parents, Lucy and Frank Forges, at 32nd Avenue and Pecos Street on the North Side, and they were there when I was born in 1954.

I've been blessed to have such a wonderful extended family, with my mom's family living in Colorado, my dad's family living in New Jersey, and others living in Colorado. I cherish the memories of growing up with Uncle Vito and Aunt Florence and spending time with my Colorado cousins. I loved the trips to New Jersey to be with my uncles, aunts, and cousins.

My dad was brought into active duty again and was in the service until 1958.

My brother, Anthony, was born when I was three years old, and my sister, LuAnn, came along four years after that.

In late 1957, shortly after Anthony was born, we moved to 36th and Tejon, across the street from Carbone's and Lechuga's, two of the area's landmark restaurants. My mom stayed home until all the kids had started school.

(Those locations won't mean much to those who weren't raised in Denver, but I know that a lot of folks who passed through Denver or still live there are lighting up and thinking . . . *Carbone's!* It's also fashionable to call the increasingly *yuppified* and gentrified North Denver something else now: The Highlands. To me, that just means you pay a quarter-million more for a house than you would otherwise.)

Mancinelli's Italian Market was an old grocery store at 32nd and Osage, and one of my first memories is going in there and seeing the cheeses hanging and Tony Mancinelli weighing out the sausage. That was our neighborhood.

After his discharge, Dad worked for a luggage company and then grocery stores for a long time. Eventually he switched to Walgreen's and was a foreman at the warehouse until they moved the warehouse to Arizona. Rather than uproot the family, he stayed in Denver and went to work for Penny Saver's Drugs.

My mom was a teacher's aide at John Dewey Junior High School and then worked at Kmart before starting to help out in doctors' offices, a job she very much enjoyed and years later would prove to be of benefit for me when her chiropractor boss, John Fisher, made a crucial recommendation in the wake of the Columbine tragedy.

My parents didn't enjoy idleness. In retirement, my dad drove a courtesy van for car dealer John Medved, and my mom worked at a local Italian restaurant, Papa J's, for thirteen years. She was heartbroken when the owners shut it down. They retired at ages eighty-six and eighty-three, respectively. I think it's in my DNA to never be fully retired. I owe everything to my parents. They've been great role models.

Even as I was growing up and attending Mount Carmel Grade School, the neighborhood was changing. Descendants of the immigrants moved away to the suburbs, but we still knew the families across the streets and across the alleys, and we would end up at their friends' dinner tables without even needing to ask, knowing the favors would be returned. If you got into trouble two blocks over, your parents knew about it. There was no hiding. Everybody knew everybody.

Rick DeBell lived a few blocks away. We started kindergarten together and quickly became inseparable.

Rick DeBell

66 *Of course, when we were in roll call and in the seating chart, it was always 'DeAngelis' and 'DeBell.' That's how it started. I was like Frank's stepbrother. Tony was the biological brother, but Frank and I were like twins. We stuck together and made it tough on Tony, and Lou and Evelyn treated me as the other son. I was there for the Sunday dinners, the family dinners, the old Italian traditional spaghetti dinners. There was a place for me. And the same thing for Frank, vice versa, when he was at our house. Sundays or birthdays, there was always a place for Frank. Our parents knew each other through church as well. We pushed each other. We were always talking about being Mantle and Maris when we played on the sandlot. At school, Frank always had to be the first to learn his multiplication tables, had to be the first to his know his states and capitols, had to be the first to have cursive penmanship—and by the way, his penmanship to this day is second to none, I have to say. He always wanted to be the first to accomplish the tasks. If we were brothers, I was Sonny Corleone, and he was Michael.* 99

On Tejon Street, we lived next door to the Ciancio family, and patriarch Joe was a legend. Pam Ciancio and I attended Mount Carmel together, and both of us nearly drowned when taking swimming lessons. "Gumba Joe," my godfather, was the councilman for District 9 and was in charge of Denver Parks and Recreation. If you've ever seen the movie, *Sandlot,* that was growing up for me. In sports, I played in the area's famous Roughriders youth football program, and Old Timers Baseball at Rocky Mountain Park.

During the summer, the kids of the neighborhood would go out in the morning and come home at night. But we weren't getting into trouble; we found things to do.

Anthony DeAngelis

"Most kids today don't even know what alleys are. But in our alleys, we used to play kickball, baseball, football—you name it. And we used to think the alleys were big. Now you go through them and say, 'How did we play anything?' But that's what we did from the time we got up in the summer. Our life revolved around sports in the alleys. Luckily, all the neighbors liked us, so they didn't have a problem if we went into their yards to retrieve balls or anything. Growing up in North Denver at that time was so fun. The parents would get on to you when you did bad stuff, but they were sort of like second parents in a way. They watched out for you too. And we played behind Carbone's sometimes. It was a dirt parking lot. We'd play Wiffle ball, and if you hit it on the top of the roof, it was a home run."

Rick DeBell

"If you hit it on the roof, that was the upper deck at Yankee Stadium."

LuAnn DeAngelis Dwyer

"Growing up there off Tejon Street, there were no girls around to play with, so the only way I got to play was if I was third base. Well, I didn't play third base. I literally was third base. That was Frank."

There were times when it was just Anthony and me playing one-on-one football in the yard. I'd be the Chicago Bears' Gale Sayers on offense and Dick Butkus on defense. My brother would be the Green Bay Packers' Paul Hornung on offense and Ray Nitschke on defense.

Everybody, or so we thought, was Italian. The lawns were beautiful. The restaurants all were fantastic. I was an altar boy at Mount Carmel from about fourth grade up to ninth grade. The best part of that was getting called out of class to serve at mass.

Mass was still in Latin, which will give you an indication of how young I was, and the only Latin words I knew were, *Mea culpa, mea culpa, mea culpa* . . . I'm sorry, I'm sorry, I'm sorry. Ricky and I thought we were pulling a fast one on the priests because we mumbled or faked our way through the allegedly mandatory Latin prayers. Something tells me now that they weren't fooled by our act.

They didn't have Eucharistic ministers, and the only person that could touch the host was the priest. Rick and I would hold the metal paten when people received communion; and at times we would rub our feet on the carpet and "shock" our friends as they received communion.

Rick DeBell

66 *We called Anthony 'Antenna Tony' because he'd hide under the bed or under the couch to try and find out what we were doing. He always wanted to be in our business, and we didn't want him around, because he was younger. So we'd stage a lot of things for him or pull a lot of things on him. Little things. We'd put Ben Gay on him, pull the sheets over him, lock him out of the house. That's really the only way we were getting into trouble with Frank's mom and dad.* 99

Anthony and I almost blew up our father once. We rounded up a bunch of fireworks and hid them in our backyard incinerator. (All North Denver homes at the time had backyard incinerators.) Dad did some yard work, cut a lot of weeds and decided to burn them in the incinerator. To make sure the fire got going, he threw some gasoline on them before tossing in the match.

Boom!

The incinerator blew up. Luckily, nothing nailed Dad. He was uninjured, but it was a close call.

Anthony DeAngelis

❝ *We didn't say anything for years. But Frank said, 'How can you blame me?' I said, 'You're the older brother. You're supposed to be the responsible one. You're supposed to tell me what not to do. Obviously, you're to blame for this.'* ❞

The Rat Pack grew, and we remain friends to this day. The roll call included Ricky, Linda Pontarelli, Debbie Pugliese, Gayle DiManna, Rocky Carbone, Steve Egender, Bobby Campbell, Jerry Caruso, Mike Bucci, and John Wasinger. The one constant in my life has been my childhood friends. Even though we didn't see each other on a regular basis, I knew they always were there for me in good times and bad.

Later, as we discovered cars, we cruised Federal Boulevard, turning around at the Scotchman Drive-In. Many of us attended Catholic schools to at least begin our education. This was before the Archdiocese began a wave of school closures.

When I was in the eighth grade, my family moved just across Denver's northern boundary to unincorporated Adams County. It was about twenty blocks up Tejon, but it was outside of the Denver city limits. I continued playing football, basketball, and baseball

all through junior high and high school. Rick and I formed a good running back tandem in ninth grade for the Mount Carmel Eagles with him blocking in front of me, but that was our last year together. Once we left Mount Carmel after ninth grade, Rick went to suburban Wheat Ridge High, and I ended up at Ranum. He came to a lot of our games, and we continued to hang out when we could. Jimmy Ruscetta, Bobby Ficca, John Smaldone, and Tony Tarantino joined the Rat Pack.

Going to Ranum, with its student body of about 2,000, was quite a culture shock for me. Sports helped me make the transition, as did the fact that I was familiar with a lot of my teammates from earlier summer ball seasons. I played basketball my sophomore year. I was a tricky little point guard, displaying not much offense and a lot of defense. From there, I stuck to baseball, mostly as a second basemen, third baseman, and outfielder. I was a decent player, but I wasn't flooded with collegiate program scholarship offers. (Okay, I didn't get any, but I had a lot of fun.)

Chris Dittman

66 I remember Frank clearly when he began attending Ranum. I was the J.V. baseball coach and I got to know him. He loved baseball, and his strength was that he understood the game. He worked hard and always did what he was asked to do. His good friends, with a couple of exceptions, came to Ranum with him since they lived in the attendance area. I had Frank in some classes when he became a senior. He hung out with a few North Side kids who were also at least registered to be in my class. Frank rode to school with them every day. They would drop him off at the front of the school then they would take off to go hang out at a gas station. I initially would ask Frank where they were and he would point to the east window

of the classroom. So I walked over, looked out and watched Rocky Carbone and Goose (John Wasinger) driving up the street. They actually waved at me!

I looked up to Chris Dittman as a teacher and coach, without realizing he would become both a role model and a close friend, and I am eternally grateful for his continued support, advice, and love. Assistant principal Don Rhoda was a great help too. He was the disciplinarian. Everybody was afraid of him, yet he had the biggest heart. His example taught me that you could be tough and love kids too. Ranum was one of the top schools in the state at the time, with great music programs and everything else. One of the ironies is that it's closed now as well. (Yes, DeAngelis, the little infielder, was two-for-two on that front. Both my high schools are history.)

I have to say I rarely was a problem for my teachers or principals. There were a couple of times, though, when I slipped. Like the time Ken Dudley, a buddy of mine, got a brand-new Chevy Chevelle and convinced me to skip class to go show it off over at Marycrest, the all-girls' school. I was supposed to be in PE class, so I called my mom, told her I wasn't feeling well, and asked her to please call Ranum later and excuse the absence.

We went over to Marycrest to wave at the girls. The folks there recognized us and called the Ranum assistant principal, Mr. Rhoda. Then Mr. Rhoda got this call from my mom, who said, "Frank wasn't feeling well, please excuse his absence from physical education." And Mr. Rhoda said, "That's interesting, since he was feeling good enough to go visit the girls at Marycrest."

So I got into trouble in school at Ranum, *and* I got grounded when I got home. I had to go to Marycrest and apologize to the administration there. Yes, all of that just for a joyride past the school in my buddy's new car.

That's an example of how times have changed. Parents supported teachers, and they never questioned coaches.

The only other time I got into trouble was a senior prank, pulled off right before we were going to play in the state baseball tournament. Our plan was to "toilet paper" the school and strategically place "For Sale" signs. Most pranks start out innocently, and that one did too. But other kids went beyond the fun and spray-painted the building.

Although we weren't involved with the spray-painting, the majority of the baseball team—including Bobby Blaser, Ray Jamsay, Darrell Herr, Pat Kennedy, Steve Meyer, John Monoco, Rick Sabell and Bruce Stoeklen—was there. My North Denver *paisano*, Rocky Carbone, assured me, "Frank, I have this great hiding place; they'll never find us." So I went with him. The rest of the baseball team took off running. The next thing I knew, Rocky and I were standing there in our "great hiding place" with our hands up.

The first person they called was Mr. Rhoda, and I had never seen him that angry. It was almost midnight when he showed up at the school and called my parents. He told me, "I'm holding you responsible for this."

The next day, I got called into the coaches' office. Coach Jim Jenkins and Coach Dittman said they'd really had to think about whether I would be allowed to go to the state tournament.

They made me sweat.

I ended up going and playing.

I like to say I wasn't much trouble. I was no angel, either, and I probably made some choices I would have chewed out my Columbine students for. But all of it—the good times and the times that led to me getting grounded—helped make me who I am. The same is true for all of us.

Part of the deal growing up was sharing a room with Anthony. My little brother, the one I am so close to now, is the most loyal brother you'll ever find. But sharing a room with him tested us throughout my teenage years, especially when Anthony felt left out.

Anthony DeAngelis

66 *Rick DeBell and Frank nicknamed me 'The Detective' because I always used to turn them in. Frank and Ricky should have been brothers. They were so close. They wouldn't let me hang out with them because they were three years older than I was. I used to terrorize them. If I had a baseball bat in my hand, whatever I had, I'd go after them. They'd torment me so bad, if I had a shoe, I'd throw my shoe at them. Anything.*

"When Frank and Ricky got older and went to Metro State College (both were living at home), they used to hang out at Super Cue, a billiards place off Federal, and they'd go there to play pool and pinball. As most Italian parents are, mine could be overprotective. Remember, we didn't have cellphones, so sometimes my parents would say, 'Let's go for a ride,' and they'd go to the Super Cue and say, 'Tony, go inside and tell Frank we're not home; we're leaving, dinner is in the oven.' Of course, I'd go in, and they'd be smoking. I'd tell them we were going for a ride, and they'd say to me, 'Don't tell your parents!' Of course, I would go outside and say, 'Guess what? They're all smoking inside!' This is what little brothers do. I would make it look like someone was sleeping in his bed when he came home, and if he had drunk a little bit, it would scare the crap out of him. As a brother, Frank was a pretty good sport most of the time, as much as I basically tortured him. 99

LuAnn DeAngelis Dwyer (to Anthony)

" You're lucky he's still talking to you, honey. "

Chapter Two

College . . . and Beyond

I was crazy about my high school girlfriend, Diane Wethington. We started going together when I was sixteen and she was fifteen.

Diane DeAngelis

  “ It was after gym class, and someone said, 'There's two guys at the bottom of the stairs, and they both like you, and you need to pick which one you like.' I came down the stairs, and I knew the other one was kind of a bad boy, and I had just been going with a bad boy, so I was looking for a decent guy. I knew Frank was a decent guy. Plus, he drove a purple Duster. ”

Our first date was Friday, November 20, 1970, to a Ranum-Westminster football game. After that, we went to the prom, to homecoming, to everything. After I graduated, I said I wanted to get married as soon as she finished high school the next year. I was an over-possessive Italian and still very immature.

Diane DeAngelis

He was so nice. He wrote me cards and took me to nice places. We spent a lot of time together in high school. He was playing baseball, he worked, I worked, and we spent all of our spare time together. We probably should have gone out with our friends more. But he was such a good guy. His mom gave me a hope chest full of stuff. He gave me a promise ring. And it just scared the bejeebers out of me. I said, 'Well, why don't we wait three or four years, or five or six,' and he said, 'Well, what about seven or eight?'

Diane broke my heart. She decided that, with me going to college, she wanted to enjoy her senior year. So she basically dumped me. Later, when she got married, she invited my parents to the wedding and they went. My parents loved Diane.

I was so crushed, I considered becoming a priest. No kidding. I checked into how to get into a seminary.

Anthony DeAngelis

He'd had other girlfriends before, but Diane was it. Diane was his true love. He was smitten. She broke his heart. I'm like, 'Frank, it's a girl. Come on.' He was so depressed for a long time. At that point, he was eighteen and I was fifteen, and I thought he was going to become a priest. We would make fun of him about it—as we still do—because I nicknamed him, 'The Padre.' The name stuck.

LuAnn DeAngelis Dwyer

It was heartbreaking for us when they broke up because we thought for sure they'd get married.

Guess what? I didn't become a priest.

I worked part-time at a couple of pizza places, Carbone's and Jim's, and Shutto grocery store while in high school and continued that when I started college at Metro State in downtown Denver. I played fall baseball right away and mostly attended night classes, at first thinking I was headed for a career in accounting. Dropping baseball, I plugged along for two years without much enthusiasm. I was starting to hang out more and more with Anthony, as we became friends as much as brothers. Rick DeBell and I were going to Metro State together, and that was gratifying. Rick was planning on getting into law school, and he was playing baseball, but he wasn't having a lot of fun pursuing a law degree.

Rick DeBell

66 We were taking things like anthropology classes, and we had no idea what we were doing. 99

One day in a cost accounting class, the professor said we all needed to subscribe to the *Wall Street Journal*. Not just that. Read it too. I had a flash: *That's it. I'm out of here.* I realized I was fooling myself because my heart wasn't in it.

I quit school and continued to work at Shutto's for about six months. I was frozen foods manager, I was a clerk, and I stocked shelves on the graveyard shift. And I asked myself, *Is this what I want to do with the rest of my life?*

Chris Dittman

66 I taught at Ranum for ten years and I loved the school. I particularly liked the class of 1972—Frank's class. I loved the kids. Frank was very well-liked by students, teachers, and coaches. He rarely if ever missed school. I didn't talk to him

much for a couple of years after he graduated. One day I ran into him and asked how he was doing and what he was majoring in. When he told me it was accounting, I asked him what the hell he was thinking. He was a born teacher, and I knew he wanted to coach. He and his best friend, Ricky, chose to switch to education, and the rest is history. 🙶

Rick DeBell

🙶 *One day we were at the White Spot having coffee and I said, 'You know what? Let's be educators! Let's go into teaching.' Honest to God, it registered with both of us, and that's how our careers came to be. Frank eventually became an administrator, of course, and I went into special education, which is as tough as it gets in education.* 🙶

I got serious about school from then on, going to Metro State during the day and delivering the *Rocky Mountain News* papers, doing filing chores for a doctor, and doing other odd jobs. Also at Metro State, Rick met his future wife, Debbie Genaro. Ricky and I have been together since we were five, and you know how I feel about Ricky. But Debbie and I have been friends since we were eighteen, and she always has been a great support to me and my family. I was best man at Ricky and Debbie's wedding and am godfather to their daughter Natalie. I was even there—accidentally—in the delivery room when she was born. I was looking for Rick at Lutheran Hospital and walked into the delivery room area. Rick was in his gown preparing to witness his daughter being born. He saw me and said, "Frank, we appreciate your support, but would you mind waiting outside?" We still laugh about that episode today.

Years later, I officiated Natalie's wedding to Josh Hotchkiss. I also watched Debbie and Ricky's younger daughter, Ashley, grow up.

When we made the decision to get our teaching certificates, Rick and I knew we would never earn as much as we might have if we had continued in accounting or law. But we also knew that being a teacher or coach would allow us to succeed in other ways. I thought back to my teacher Chris Dittman and the impact he'd had on my life, and I decided I wanted to be like him. I wanted to be a teacher and a coach. That decision changed everything for me. And I've since experienced what Chris Dittman must have known all along: You can't put a price on the feeling you get when a student tells you that you have had an impact on his or her life.

I was a couple of years behind graduating with my class because I had changed my majors. I was living at my parents' house, and the pact was that as long as I was going to school, I could stay with them … as long as I graduated during the twentieth century.

My siblings were surprised by, or at least misunderstood, my career choice.

LuAnn DeAngelis Dwyer

❝ Realistically, I couldn't picture him as a teacher. But I always knew how much he cared about people. ❞

Anthony DeAngelis

> *I figured he was doing it because of sports—he wanted to coach. I figured he was going to end up like our old PE teachers: do nothing, let the kids go lift weights, and coach.*

I fooled them!

I ended up getting my degree from Metro State and even started coaching football and baseball with Rick and Rocky in a Denver parks program while in school. I did my student teaching and coached at Jefferson High in Edgewater, just across Denver's west border in Jefferson County. I liked it there and would have stayed on, but there were no jobs available.

LuAnn DeAngelis Dwyer

> *Frank, at the time, was very quiet. So when he was student teaching and I was in high school, I was thinking he was too quiet. But I became friends with some of the kids from Jefferson, and they're like, 'Oh, my God, he's the best; you should hear him!' I was like, 'Really? Around me he says, like, two words.'*

Living with Anthony and LuAnn, I never got the opportunity to talk. Why? Because they never shut up!

After graduation, I taught as a substitute in the fall term and was hired to help coach football under Greg Springston at Wheat Ridge High. Rick DeBell helped coach there for a year as well, and so the inseparable buddies were together one final time before Rick moved on to Aurora Central. (Rick stayed in the Aurora Public Schools, spending a majority of his career as a special education teacher at Kenton Elementary until he retired in 2014.) One of the assistant football coaches for the Wheat Ridge Farmers was Joe Newman, the head baseball coach. He asked me if I wanted to help coach baseball, and I said, "Sure!" I ended up getting a limited contract, teaching psychology the second half of that year while I coached under Newman. The familiar problem was that when my temporary contract was up, there wasn't a full-time opening. But I was committed to continue coaching at Wheat Ridge while substitute teaching. I really liked the school and the administrators and coaches for whom I was working. Greg and Joe were great mentors for me as I began my coaching career.

At the time, I didn't even know where Columbine High was. I was a North Denver kid. I didn't even know there was life on the south side of Colfax. Columbine is *waaaay* south of Colfax in an unincorporated area of Jefferson County. Although Columbine's mailing address is Littleton, that's misleading. Littleton is the seat of Arapahoe County, and Columbine is about five miles west of Littleton's downtown. I'm guessing that until 1999, most Denver-area residents thought of the Columbine area as being in the Jefferson County city of Lakewood, not Littleton. That's understandable. Columbine is a Jefferson County school, the Rebels mostly played in the Jeffco leagues in sports (until metro-area alignment was juggled to get like-sized schools in each league), and the Lakewood boundary is nearby. That's a long way of saying that to those familiar with the Denver area, it never has sounded right, before or after 1999, to say that Columbine is "in" Littleton. Here's another frame of reference: The high school is fourteen miles southwest of the Colorado State Capitol building in downtown Denver.

Columbine High opened in 1973, and its first senior class graduated in 1975.

In late August 1979, I got a call from Columbine principal Terry Conley, who said they needed a social studies teacher and assistant baseball coach for the "Track A" that started in late October. Columbine, at the time, was one of the Jeffco schools operating on a year-round schedule. I went down for an interview, and it was Conley, me, and nobody else.

Conley told me they liked what they saw of me when Wheat Ridge played Columbine in baseball, and he understood I was a good teacher, qualified for the opening. He later said this in a *Denver Post* profile story about me: "I saw him with his team and the way he handled them, the care that he demonstrated. That's why, in my opinion, they were such a good team. If he talked to them, he left them confident."

I told Mr. Conley (and he was *Mr.* Conley to me at the time) thanks, but that the football season was on the verge of starting at Wheat Ridge. I was all in with those kids and that staff, and I didn't think I should bail out on them to take the Columbine job.

Conley, a former coach himself, understood and appreciated my loyalty. He also argued that, for my own sake, I needed to take a full-time teaching job. There was no guarantee of when the next position would open up or that I'd get it. This was going to be my foot in the door to a full-time career.

Thankfully, the two staffs had worked it out so that I could teach at Columbine and still coach football at Wheat Ridge. It took cooperation and flexibility in scheduling (the schools are about a half-hour drive apart), but it was doable. And we managed it.

Finally, I was a full-time educator. I was all the way up to earning $11,000 a year. I bought a townhouse near Bear Creek High School in Lakewood. At one point, I even coached the freshman basketball team. When I protested that a five-foot, six-inch former guard wasn't an appropriate coach, Conley told me, "I'm not asking you to coach the centers."

There was a bump in the road when I had to move to Deer Creek Junior High for one year, in 1980–81, when they made

Columbine a three-year school rather than four. But after only a year, Columbine had another social studies' teaching opening, and I went back to the high school. Principal Warren Hanks hired me to teach social studies, and Merle Wicklund hired me to work with head football coach Sherm Pruitt as defensive coordinator in football and as head baseball coach after only a year at Deer Creek. I count Deer Creek in my Columbine stay because it was a feeder school, and the assignment was temporary. It made me a better teacher.

I was a Columbine Rebel. Little did I realize I was a Rebel for life!

Anthony DeAngelis

" *I quickly saw that Frank was the kind of coach who would get on to a kid, but then he was also the first one to pat him on the back. It was that kind of relationship. He was there for them. I figured that one day, he wouldn't be just a teacher; he would move up. Now, how far he would move up, I didn't know. I thought he would be a principal somewhere just because he cared so much about the kids. To this day, when some people talk about my brother, a lot of times they'll say, 'Oh, that's just a front.' It is not a front. That is so much him. He still cares about kids.* "

Chapter Three

Columbine: Early Days

I dived into my work at Columbine.

Initially I was social studies teacher and coach as well as the public address announcer at a lot of the boys' and girls' basketball games and wrestling matches.

I wasn't very good at saying "no" to anyone. I was so involved as a sponsor for various groups and activities and as a coach that Warren Hanks would take my keys on Friday and tell me he didn't want to see me back at school until Monday. That was my life at the time. The principal had to kick me out of the school for the weekend.

Later when I became mentor to a lot of teachers and principals, I would say, "Do as I say, not as I do." If I had one thing to do over, it would be to balance out my personal and professional life. My job consumed everything.

Tom Tonelli

❝ I've known Frank (it's actually hard for me to call him Frank because he will always be Coach De to me) since I was fourteen years old. He was my American history teacher, and I played football for him when I was at Columbine in the late eighties. I think when De was a teacher, he ran his classes a lot like the way he ran the school once he became principal. It was also the same way he coached. By that I mean that he was always really prepared. He understood what was going on in the classroom and on the field. He was very knowledgeable about curriculum as a teacher and district policy as an administrator. And when he coached, there was never any doubt from his players about his understanding of the game. That is why when he talked, we all listened. In each of those fields—teaching, administration, and coaching—there are men and women who have those same qualities. What was impressive was that De could do all those things and build solid, meaningful, and enduring relationships at the same time. Still, how good De was never really sunk in until I entered the field of education. Once I had that perspective, I knew that what made De different was the same thing that makes other teachers stand out. And that is their ability to convey not only how much they know but also how much they care. I think that is why students at Columbine loved De and why his players all felt like we would run through a brick wall for him. ❞

As the football defensive coordinator from 1981–93 and baseball coach for the Rebels from 1982–94, I was part of two state championships. Both were in baseball, in '87 and '91. Both times we were underdogs. We beat Skyline High School of Longmont, which was undefeated in '87, and in '91 we beat Pueblo South in the championship game at historic Damon Runyon Field down in Pueblo. The Colts hadn't lost in something like two years. My coaching career ended in 1994 when I became an administrator because those were the district rules.

Back then the kids played more than one sport. Most of them played two, and a lot played three. Many of the kids I coached in football were baseball players too. In football, they'd confide in me as the assistant, and then I'd be their head coach in baseball. I got to know them. In the summer, I would coach summer league baseball and do weight training for football. What I realized early in my coaching career is that the better the players, the better coach I was. They made me look good. I worked with great student-athletes. The accomplishments of the players on the field made me happy, but what made me extremely proud was the fine men they became. They are great husbands and fathers and great human beings.

People still ask me which sport I liked coaching the most. They're surprised to hear it was football. I loved baseball, but being an assistant coach—in any sport—you get to coach. You just coach. The terrific head coaches I worked under, Sherm Pruit, Bob Asleson and Dennis Eckley, allowed me to coach. And as a head coach in baseball, there was so much more that went with it, such as fundraising. I got to coach, but at the same time, I didn't have the same opportunities I had as an assistant.

I had two long-time baseball assistants, Rick Bath and Karl Nitta, and I always will cherish the time I spent coaching with my dear friend Dave Sanders. Dave and I both were emotional in my last game against Tom Severtson and Denver East in 1994. Once again, the coaches who succeeded me as head coaches—Jud Blatchford, Robin Ortiz, Chuck Gillman and Brooks Roybal— always welcomed me with open arms and never made me feel as if

I was meddling. I worked with three outstanding athletic directors during my principalship: Kevin Land, my North Denver buddy Ed Woytek, and Scott Christy. A leadership lesson I learned early in my career was to surround myself with great people and build a team that had a common vision.

I still was considered a "player's coach" who cared as much about our players away from the diamond as on it, and that was an extension of my approach in the classroom, the hallways, and anywhere else involving those kids. Many of our players went on to college baseball, and a few were taken in the Major League Baseball draft, and it was common to see former Rebels in the stands for games and some back to help me coach. It also heartened me when Tom Tonelli joined the staff as a social studies teacher and coach in 1994 after his graduation from the University of Colorado-Denver just as I was moving into administration.

Chris Dittman

66 *I was a baseball umpire and worked several of Frank's games over the years. He was an outstanding coach. He was a players' coach and treated his kids with respect and dignity. That didn't surprise me because that's how he treated everyone.* 99

I had gotten married in 1985 and adopted my wife Cheryl's two children, Bryant and Hayley, as my stepchildren. I became a husband and a father for the first time. It was life changing. It was great to have a family. Bryant was eight years old and Hayley was eight months when Cheryl and I started dating in 1984. After we married I enjoyed being a husband and father. Bryant started high school at Chatfield but transferred to Columbine his sophomore year. It was great having Bryant at Columbine. I enjoyed coaching him in football and baseball, but his best sport was wrestling and he finished sixth at the state meet as a senior. We moved to Highlands Ranch when Hayley was in elementary school. Hayley went to Douglas County schools, getting involved in many activities. She was a sophomore at ThunderRidge High School on April 20, 1999. After my marriage in 1985, I tried to balance my personal and professional life, and I still feel I didn't do a good job. Nine years later, I finally conceded to give up teaching to move up. I sought advice from a lot of folks, including Rick, who had settled into his career at Aurora Central.

Rick DeBell

❝I always thought that Frank was capable of leading on a larger scale. He asked me, 'What do you think? Should I go into administration?' I said, 'Absolutely. You'd be great at it.'❞

I know a lot of educators leave the classroom because they're bored. I wasn't. I loved the kids. They are the reason I got into education. When an administrator told me I'd be a good fit for the front office, I responded, "Why would I want to be one of you?" I was only half-kidding. The comeback to my question hit home with me. As a teacher, I might have a hundred and fifty kids, maybe a few more than that as a coach. But as an administrator, I could impact the lives of *two thousand* kids.

So when my then principal and mentor, Ron Mitchell, mentioned that there would be an opening for assistant principal, I went to the University of Phoenix in Denver and earned my administrative license. In the spring of 1994, I became an assistant principal. I served as interim athletic director in 1991, which gave me administrative experience. From 1993-95 I was dean of students and assistant principal/activities director, setting the stage for me to become a principal.

Anthony DeAngelis

66 *There'd be times I'd stop in and go to lunch with him. I was amazed how he could walk down the hall and there would be all these kids coming down the hallway, and it would be, 'Hey, Bobby,' 'Hey, Mary,' . . . and this was when he was assistant principal. They weren't kids he had in a class. He said, 'I know just about all the kids. Now, some of the freshmen, it takes me a while to get their names, but I know just about every kid in this school.'* 99

Although I couldn't coach, I still hung around the football program as much as was practical. I am eternally grateful to Andy Lowry, who was hired as Columbine's head coach in 1994. I was going through coaching withdrawal, and he allowed me to remain active with the team. (Andy still is Columbine's coach as of this writing. He teased me by calling me the Jerry Jones of Columbine football, and there's no doubt he soon will be a Colorado Hall of Fame coach.) He is not only a great coach, but also is a great human being who cares about his players on and off the field. Many of his players are coaching for him, and he has surrounded himself with great assistant coaches,

The Columbine principal's job opened up in the summer of 1996. I wanted the job, but I was concerned that two of my close friends and long-time assistant principals, Dr. Maria Reschke and Kevin Land, might want it. There was no way I was going to apply for the job if either of them wanted it. I would support them and work with them. I cherish loyalty and it would have been an honor to work for them. They both came to me and said they weren't going to apply, so that opened the door for me.

When I interviewed for the position, a few people at the district level expressed concern that I had spent my entire full-time career at Columbine. I'd only been an assistant principal for a couple of years, and they wondered if it would be difficult for me to take the lead because I was friendly with a lot of the people I would be supervising.

Later I learned that the other finalist was Chris Dittman, who by then was the principal at Westminster High, north of Denver. I was going against the man who inspired me to get into teaching and coaching. I told myself that this couldn't be any better. I looked at it as going through the interview for the experience. My assumption was that I would be going to work for the guy I idolized. We ended up being scheduled for final interviews back-to-back. There we were, sitting outside the room, waiting together. They called Mr. Dittman in first, and what he did next amazed me: He walked in and announced that I should get the job, in part because, unlike him, I was entrenched at Columbine.

Chris Dittman

❝I had been recruited to apply for the Columbine principal's job when Ron Mitchell announced he was retiring. As fate would have it I was one of the two finalists. The other was Frank DeAngelis. I'm a North Side guy but was interested because of Columbine's reputation in academics and athletics. As I sat in the final interview with staff, students, and parents, one of the parents asked me why they should hire me. I thought for a moment and then gave an answer I believed strongly. I said there are three things a principal has to have to be successful: staff support, student support, and parent support. I told them they had a man waiting to interview with them that already possessed all of those necessities. I said, 'He might not have the experience I have as a principal, but those three support groups won't let him fail.' They didn't and he *didn't. Frank is one of the few people in education who could have withstood that tragic 1999 day and stuck with the kids, parents, and staff. They stuck by him as well.* 🙺

Tom Tonelli

🙶 *When I came back to Columbine after college, I had a deeper appreciation of De. It's not that I didn't love him before. But it's a little bit like what I've heard about kids when they're leaving for college. When they leave for college, they don't think their father knows much, and when they get done with college, they think their father knows it all. Well, I have a great dad, but De has been a father figure in my life too. We stayed in touch when I was at school. And there was no way he wasn't going to get an invitation to my wedding. He was there for me that day. Like always. When I came back to teach, I had such an appreciation for him and what he had done for me. I think a lot of the staff felt that same way. That is why when the principal job opened, we all thought he was the guy who should get it. Of course, we knew there was going to be a hiring committee, but everyone I knew wanted De. It wasn't just because he was committed to Columbine, but all of us thought he would be a great principal. And he was.* 🙺

I got the job.

Chapter Four

The Big Office

In those first few years, I forged my philosophy as a principal.

It was sobering when Ron Mitchell told me: "Frank, I don't care if you were an assistant principal for twenty years or two years; until you're the one sitting behind that desk making decisions, you have no idea what it's going to be like." And that was true. A lot of times, you deal with certain things as an assistant principal, but as a principal, you have to deal with the entire organization. You're dealing with staff and assistant principals and with facility maintenance and food service people. If people are unhappy, their complaints end up on your desk. You get those phone calls and emails.

Ron was right when he told me that I had to work with three different groups: staff members, students, and parents. His warning was that if I worked well with only one or two groups, I could survive, but it would be difficult. The key to a long and successful career, he said, was to get the support of all three groups. I knew Chris Dittman had a similar philosophy. That was a challenge, for sure, but I was never one to shy away from a challenge.

I had a lot of anxiety initially because of the potential awkwardness. The faculty members had wanted me to apply. Gordon Hayes and Ryan West were two of my dear friends, and they were on the interview committee and offered encouragement to me during the entire process. The community had wanted me to apply, but as I've noted, there were those skeptics in district administration that wondered whether my experience was too narrow.

Anthony DeAngelis

    ❝ *Going by the usual rules, that principalship probably shouldn't have been his at that time. But the Columbine parents really pushed for him because they knew him. We looked at it like it was going to be great either way because if he didn't get the post, he'd be working for Chris Dittman. I think he knew how privileged he was to have that job, and he was not going to let anybody down. He said, 'I will learn, and we will do this together.'* ❞

I nervously prepared for my first faculty meeting when the staff returned in August. A lot of those people had mentored me, and I had worked for them in their departments. I jokingly told some staff members they probably would have been nicer to me if they knew I'd be their boss one day. I was fortunate to have such a great staff as I began my first—and what turned out to be my only—principalship. But my nerves settled as the meeting took on a family atmosphere. When I finished speaking, someone said, "It was like you were in the locker room, preparing the team to go out and play a game." The coach in me really came out, and that wasn't going to stop.

I was smart enough to know that I wasn't going to make a lot of changes right away. It was a great school. We wanted to carry on the excellence that had been established. I was only the fifth principal at Columbine since 1973, and I wanted to build on the school's traditions and strengths.

I had earned a lot of credibility with the teachers because I had taught for fifteen years. A few teased me when I moved into administration by saying, "Are you going to become one of *them*?" But one of the biggest compliments paid to me years later when I retired was, "You never were one of them; you were one of us." That was important. It stuck with me when a colleague and friend, Susan Peters, told me, "Frank, your position is changing, but you don't have to change." She emphasized that I needed to stick with what had made me successful as a teacher and as an assistant principal, and what a great challenge it was to shape the lives of two thousand kids. I was determined to prove that I could do that. It was all about relationships.

My biggest worry was that once I became an administrator, I would lose the relationships and interactions I had with kids. I had been involved with the students and the kids through teaching and coaching ever since I had gotten into education, and I didn't want that to change.

I also realized that the job would demand some things that I was not used to; for example, dealing with the bureaucracy—education gives government a run for its money there—and attending and running all those meetings. There's always another meeting.

I quickly established myself as an activist principal. I wasn't going to sit in my office. One of the things I did from the start was to block out an hour or two a day to spend time in the classrooms with the teachers and the kids. I hung out in the hallway and cafeteria. I used to tell my staff that if they wanted to talk to me, they could set up an appointment because I wanted to be with the kids. At the same time, I felt that it was important to be as much a confidant and friend to members of the faculty as it was to be a boss. As principal I tried to live by what motivational speaker Brian Tracy says: "Become the kind of leader that people would follow voluntarily, even if you had no title or position."

Students got used to me wandering the halls, taking part in school assemblies, and showing up for activities of all kinds. People assumed that because I was a former coach, I was going to support athletics. And I did; but I didn't miss a school play or musical, either. I supported them too. Before long, I could hum along to the songs in *Fiddler on the Roof*, *Bye Bye Birdie*, and *Oklahoma*.

Being present and active in the school gave me an edge. If a parent called up and said, "Frank, I have a complaint about a teacher," I could say, "That's interesting; I've been in that classroom several times, and what your son or daughter is telling us is not what I'm observing in there."

Yes, there were some who held my coaching background against me. It went farther back than when I was principal too. There were staffers and community members who believed great teachers were teachers only and that coaches were just filling time during the school day if they were in the classroom until practice began. I took that personally.

One of the jokes went like this:

Question: "What's the first name of all the teachers in the social studies department?"

Answer: "Coach."

Yet many of the most successful teachers we had at Columbine were coaches. They were adept at organizing and managing their time. Because of that stereotype that coaches couldn't be great teachers, I was always out to prove them wrong . . . and I still was when I moved up to principal.

The relationships I had in coaching carried over to my relationships with students, and all of that helped me make the transition to principal. As principal, I told myself that I never would hire a coach based solely on his or her win and loss record. He or she had to be a good teacher. I also thought it was important to have coaches in the building during the day, not just getting there in the afternoon. If you have coaches who aren't there as teachers, they're not working with students in classrooms or perhaps the gym. I looked to hire great teachers, and if they could coach, that was a bonus.

Tom Tonelli

66 *Frank was a principal who loved athletics. That was true. But it's so unfair to say De favored athletes or coaches. If anything, those guys were on the radar and more was expected from them. I knew Frank as the guy who cared, but he cared about my friends that were male and female and those who didn't play sports as much as the athletes. That's what people who weren't at Columbine don't know. They don't know that as a principal, De went to everything. Yes, he was at sporting events, but you'd also find him at every single play, at every single choir concert, at speech and debate competitions; in fact, that's the biggest issue that I have with De: The job was too much a part of his identity. It became so much of who he was, and I honestly wish that he hadn't felt that pressure.* 99

I had a bit of a honeymoon period that first year. I knew that. At that first commencement, in 1997, I told the kids they'd always have a special place in my heart. One of the advantages I had was that even though the Class of '97 was my first graduating class, I knew those kids. I talked about them as freshmen from back when I still was teaching. And then I was the student senate sponsor for the following two years, and I knew a lot of those kids. I could say, "Gosh, I remember when you walked through that door with your eyes wide open as freshmen, and now you're seniors, ready to take on the world."

So I was a first-year principal, but it wasn't my first year with those kids. I had always been Mr. De or Coach De, and that didn't change when I became principal. As I got older, they called me Papa De.

In the second year, the honeymoon was over, and things finally felt solid.

No longer nervous, I enjoyed the first-day-back pep talk to the faculty that August. I gave my state of the school, the Rebel Address, and I wanted to motivate them and talk about passion for the job. So, yeah, it took me back to my coaching days.

Later, when a teacher was about to retire, he confessed to me that in his first few years at Columbine, during my talks about family and togetherness, he would sit there and mumble that he wasn't buying "this crap." Then he said that as he was leaving the job, he knew he *was* leaving his family. I think a lot of people believe you can't create that sense of family and belonging at a large school. You can. You can let the kids know you care about them. I used to tell teachers, "They don't care how much you know until they know how much you care." I remember someone telling me, "One good adult can make all the difference." It's true. You can't underestimate the impact you can have as a teacher or staff member on students. Each day you walk into a classroom, you can make a difference in a child's life. Family was the creed I was raised on, and I was convinced that each member of our Columbine family contributed to the success of our school.

As the time went on, I realized having many staff members I had known for years was a great advantage, not a cause for concern. The staff members who had been with me never tried to take advantage of our friendship. We had a special bond and had developed a mutual respect. They knew my door was always open.

There were times I did not agree with them, or they didn't get what they wanted, but they knew their voices were heard, and I treated them consistently and fairly. I had a teacher's union representative jokingly say, "You are too nice to your staff members. They feel they don't need to join the union because they know they will be treated fairly." I took that as a compliment. In my eighteen years as principal, I can count on one hand the number of union grievances that were filed against me.

When I interviewed a candidate or sat in on an interview, it bothered me if the person spent the interview talking about himself or herself and their degree and this or that award. I never asked, "What's your feeling about kids?" Because no one is going to say, "I can't stand them." What I listened for, instead, was how they talked about kids, about helping them, and about inclusiveness. That's how I found the right people to bring into our family.

I loved my job, so it bothered me when I would have teachers come up to me and say, "Frank, I only have fourteen more Mondays." Or, "I have only five more faculty meetings where I have to listen to you." I promised myself that I never wanted to get to a point in my career where I was counting the days. Well, I was wrong. I eventually did get to that point, but it wasn't about counting down the days; it was about savoring the moments. I knew how much I going to miss it.

My second year as principal marked the first of what would become an annual appearance in English classes. In costume, I portrayed colonial era theologian Jonathan Edwards delivering the famous sermon, "Sinners in the Hands of an Angry God." I knew I was pushing the envelope, given the watchdog approach of many who wanted to keep references to religion out of the schools. But I got away with it, and continued the tradition long past 1999. I always will be indebted to English teacher Paula Reed for allowing me to start the tradition. (Even in retirement, I continue to appear to sermonize in character. You can't take the Rebel—or Jonathan Edwards—out of me.)

As my third year as principal approached in the summer of 1998, I had ballooned up to 210 pounds, primarily because I had stopped working out and wasn't coaching. At my height, I looked like the Michelin Man. I went in for a physical, and my cholesterol was up over four hundred. My blood pressure went up. My doctor said, "Frank, I'm telling you right now, if you don't change some things, with the stress you're under, you're facing some serious health issues."

I joined Weight Watchers with some friends. I'm pretty type-A, so I followed everything. Within two weeks, I lost twenty-two pounds, so that shows you how badly I was abusing my health. Between August of 1998 and March of 1999, I lost sixty-five pounds. I was down to 145. My cholesterol dropped, my blood pressure was down. I started going to the gym every day before school. I'd get up at 4:30 in the morning and go work out at the Highlands Ranch Recreation Center or 24-Hour Fitness. I'd usually get to school by 6:30 each day. Because I felt the need to get to every event, I'd get home at 8:30, 9:00, or 10:00 at night.

I felt that to be effective, I had to work long hours. To me, there was no such thing as a time clock. I look back at the philosophy now, and I don't recommend it. There must be a balance between personal and professional lives.

On Friday, April 16, 1999, the eve of the junior-senior prom, I addressed an assembly, emphasizing the potential perils of the weekend. I told the students about a college friend's death in a motorcycle accident and about a Columbine baseball player's fatal crash. I told them I didn't want to attend another memorial service and told them to look around them, then close their eyes and think of losing a friend and classmate because of a choice they had made.

With their eyes still closed, I had them say after me: "I am a valued member of Columbine High School family. And I'm not in this alone."

After I told them I loved them and that I wanted to see each of their smiling faces on Monday morning, Ivory Moore led the "We are Columbine!" cheer with each side of the gym shouting its part.

On Monday, April 19, while watching our home baseball game against our rival Chatfield, one of my best friends on the faculty, teacher and girls' basketball coach Dave Sanders, sat down next to me. He was going to be at open gym that night for girls' basketball, so he was hanging around, and we started talking about our lives and our careers.

Dave had arrived at Columbine in 1977, two years before me. He mentored me as we coached basketball together with Dale McCoy and Rudy Martin. Our kids had gone to school together. He was almost always the first teacher through the doors each morning, and he'd often stop my office for a chat. Nothing heavy, nothing long, just two friends talking casually each morning.

That afternoon, somehow, the conversation felt a little different. Suddenly, Dave asked me, "You ever have any regrets about choosing the career you did and the time away from your family?"

We both said we'd do it all over again, but that we were both looking forward to our next journeys in life. He told me he was ready to spend more time with his wife, Linda, his daughters, and his grandkids.

With my third school year as principal winding down, I felt I had made my mark in the job, and I looked forward to my continuing life as a Rebel.

Chapter Five

April 20, 1999

That beautiful spring morning, I arrived at school around 10:00 after attending a Future Business Leaders of America breakfast. Several Columbine students had been recognized at the breakfast for their involvement in the program. Because of the morning meeting, I had missed my daily chat with Dave Sanders, but our discussion at the baseball game the night before was still on my mind. I couldn't have known it would be my final conversation with him, but I wish I had hugged him and told him how much I loved him.

Normally, by late morning I would have headed down to the cafeteria with my assistant principals to share supervision of the first lunch period, which started at 11:15. I loved lunch duty. It was a great way to spend time with the kids in an informal atmosphere; it provided an opportunity to be seen and to let them know I was there for them. But when the first lunch period began that morning, I still was in my office, meeting with Kiki Leyba. Kiki had been on a one-year temporary contract, teaching both English and social studies, and I was offering him a full-time English position for the following school year.

Kiki Leyba

> 66 *The day before in the hallway, Frank had asked me to come by the next morning, and I knew he was going to offer me a contract for the next year. I don't think he outright said it, but I knew things were positive, and my department chair said things were looking good. That night, my girlfriend—now my wife—and I went out to celebrate at Beau Jo's Pizza. I really was happy to be at Columbine. I'd spent some time at other schools, and I was so impressed with the things I had seen at Columbine and the people I had met. So that day, I had finished a class, and I went by Frank's office when lunch started. He had this little couch and two chairs by the door of his office, and he was kind of giving me the 'Welcome to the Rebel family' talk.* 99

At 11:19 a.m., shots rang out. My secretary and education assistant, Susan White, raced to my office so quickly that she did a little face-plant in the door before opening it and saying, "Frank, there's been a report of gunfire." The fire alarm was sounding and the strobe lights were flashing. Students and staff members were running in the halls. Others were in lockdown in classrooms.

I ran out of the office, heading toward the commons. For a few seconds, I thought it might have been a senior prank. We were a month away from graduation, and I thought a few kids were trying to scare the other students. But I quickly realized this was real, not some prank or false alarm. My worst nightmare had become a reality. *This can't be happening*, I thought.

Kiki Leyba

❝ Frank bolted out of his chair, and I followed right behind him. He made his way out to the hallway, and behind us Susan yelled, 'What should I do?' Frank was moving ahead, and I asked Frank what he wanted Susan to do, and Frank said, 'Call 911!' I yelled back to her to call 911. When we got to the front commons area, Frank was not in a full run, but he wasn't walking either. I looked down the hall and saw the silhouette of a guy holding a long gun. I could still hear gunfire, but that guy wasn't shooting. None of that made sense in the moment, but that's what I saw. I stood there watching Frank and thinking, Man, Frank is running toward gunfire. Who does that? *Then I started yelling at the kids who were in the front area to get out of there, to get outside quickly. I got a lot of puzzled and annoyed looks from students. I wasn't sure how much information to give them, but I also needed them to get out of there. ❞*

I spotted a gunman wearing a white T-shirt, dark pants, and boots coming toward me. It was Eric Harris. Dylan Klebold might have been nearby, but I saw Harris. The two killers had worn trench coats outside—a fact that led to considerable confusion and misunderstanding—to hide their weapons, but had ditched them by then. Everything seemed to move in slow motion. Harris fired shots that shattered glass behind me.

It's funny what your mind does in a crisis situation. I don't remember hearing the blare of the fire alarms. (I don't know who set off the alarms. I don't think it was Harris and Klebold, because they hadn't intended to come into the building; their plan was to shoot students and staff members as they exited the building once the bombs exploded.) I guess I blocked out the sound, but

I remember the strobe lights flashing. I also remember exactly how those shots and the glass shattering behind me sounded. I expected Harris to shoot again—to shoot me. I wondered what it was going to feel like to have a bullet pierce my body. I thought of my family. I thought about never being able to say goodbye and never seeing my family again on this side of heaven.

Just then, a group of about twenty-five girls came out of the locker room headed to physical education class. They were in front of me and had no idea what was going on or that they were heading right into the crossfire. I rushed toward them and herded them into a side hallway. I wanted to get them into the main gym and then lock the doors, but because we were in lockdown, the gym doors were already locked. Frantically, I reached into my coat pocket and pulled out my huge ring of about thirty-five keys.

In the chaos of that moment, I heard more gunshots firing. I heard panicked students scream out, "Mr. De, Mr. De!" Strobe lights flashed all around us, warning us to get out of there.

And somehow, the first key I grabbed was the one that opened the gym door.

One door, one key.

I tried to duplicate that later and couldn't. That key didn't have a special marking on it or anything. It was in the middle of the key ring and felt like all the other keys.

A lot of things happened that day that I couldn't explain, and that was one of them.

I got the girls to a storage area in the gym and told them to stay there. I said I would return once I made sure it was safe to exit the building, I told them not to open the door until I said the password. We had a brief discussion about what the password would be and after arguing back and forth, we finally decided on the phrase, "Oranges in the newspaper." I don't know where that came from, but a nervous laugh eased the tension slightly. Later

I realized we did not need a password, because I had a key to let the girls out of the storage area. The girls will always have a special place in my heart, and we have a special bond. I get tears in my eyes when they send me pictures of them with their husbands and kids and thank me for saving their lives.

We didn't know what was going on around us. I didn't have time to stop and think about why the gunman didn't keep shooting at me or at the girls in the hallway or about why he didn't chase us. Later I learned that Dave Sanders had rushed out of the faculty lounge and into the commons to warn students. He came up the commons staircase at the same time that I moved to keep the girls out of harm's way. Seeing the gunman, Dave turned away, but Harris went after him and shot him in the back, neck, and torso. One of the most difficult things for me has been the guilt of knowing that if Dave had stayed in the faculty lounge, I likely would have been a victim. One of my best friends saved my life by running towards danger to warn and save kids.

With the girls safe for the moment in the gym, I didn't want to risk taking them outside until I was sure there were no gunmen or snipers waiting there. I peeked outside the door and saw a Jeffco Sheriff's officer, Jeff White. I told him I needed to go back in the building and get the girls. I went back in, got the girls, and hurried them outside.

When I moved to go back into the building, White stopped me. He said I couldn't go back in because they were securing the perimeter. We had to wait for SWAT.

Waiting with law enforcement personnel on the street outside was agonizing. Terrified, I imagined what might be going on in the school. Everywhere I looked, kids—my kids—were crying. I felt numb.

The police took me to the mobile units they'd set up on the street by Clement Park. I knew several of the Denver police officers who were there, including David Pontarelli, Frank Vessa, Tony Yacovetta, and Vince DiManna. A lot of them already were angry about not being able to go in. They would get angrier. Bob Armstrong, a Littleton police officer and a friend and parent of former Columbine students, was there and kept me abreast of what they knew.

Kiki and I were briefly reunited at the mobile units. He told me that when I went to help the girls, he had run down the academic hallway toward the social studies and English classes, chasing out students who were hanging out in the halls during the lunch period and warning teachers in the offices.

Kiki Leyba

66 *On that day, people were kind of slow to react to anyone trying to usher them out of the building. If the same thing happened today, people wouldn't blink. They'd be gone. But then, they didn't have any context for the danger or the need to escape.*

"When I reached the doors at the end of the hallway, I remembered that my cell phone was in the car. I didn't even have it with me. Hardly anybody carried their phones on them then, and I had a phone in my classroom, so I usually didn't need it. My car was pretty close to the doors, so I ran out, grabbed my phone, and tried calling 911. I got a busy signal. I tried again, and it was busy again. I remembered the gunfire, and thought, I'm right by the front door, I shouldn't be standing here, this isn't a good spot to be. *That's when I jumped in my car and drove out of the parking lot down toward the Clement Park entrance where a lot of our students parked. I stopped the car and saw several police vehicles pull up—some stopped in the middle of Pierce Street. A few students who had returned from lunch were walking from their cars toward the building, and I told them to stay put. Then I ran over to the police and told them I was a teacher and that I had been in the school. Then, all of a sudden, Frank was next to me. I didn't even see him walk up.* 🙶

The officers had a dry erase board and asked Kiki and me if we could draw them a map of the school. They even asked if I could tell them about where the ventilation system openings were. I was both incredulous and honest enough to say I couldn't be that specific. I had a difficult time remembering the numbers on the classroom doors. (Today, of course, first responders can immediately call up school blueprints on computers.) Another officer came up and ordered Kiki to move back because they were creating a perimeter.

At one point, someone mentioned the possibility of me putting on a bulletproof vest so I could go back into the building and turn off the fire alarm. I'd have done it in a heartbeat; I wanted to get back into the school to my kids. But the idea was quickly nixed. *Nobody* was going to be allowed into the building ahead of the SWAT forces.

While I understood the need to be careful, I thought (and maybe even said), *Are you kidding me?* The theory was that storming the school might drive the killers to add to the toll or that innocent students could be caught in the crossfire. The officers wanted to get in there—to do *something*—and a few threatened to break the chain of command and go in on their own. They were angry because they had been trained to save lives, they had sworn to serve, they knew kids were in there dying, and they were being ordered *not* to enter. Some of them were parents of kids in the building. Inertia, though, was the protocol of the time.

Secure the perimeter until SWAT can go in. Those were the rules.

Tom Tonelli

Ivory Moore and I walked through the front doors to go to the teachers' parking lot. We wanted to drive over to New York Bagel for lunch. By the time we got to the restaurant, somebody had called and said that someone had a gun in the school. We drove straight back. The time between when we left and got back couldn't have more than ten minutes. Police had already arrived, kids had run from the building, and we ended up across the street from the school in Leawood Park. Pretty quickly, a lot of people—faculty and kids—got together. It was total chaos. We heard five hundred different stories— some said it was two kids; it was ten kids; they're wearing white; they're wearing black; it was this kid; no, it was that kid; it was Columbine kids; no, it's not Columbine kids; they're in this part of the building; they're in that part of the building. Asking the students what they had seen and experienced only complicated the story, so we had no idea what was really going on.

"We moved from Leawood over to Clement Park, and I saw De talking to the police. I looked at him. We just made eye contact. I'm sure he doesn't remember it, but I'll never forget the look on his face. It was the look of a man who had just lost his child in a way that he had never expected. It was a look of desperation. His worst fear, the worst fear of any father, had come true.

LuAnn DeAngelis Dwyer

" *I was at the Lakewood Country Club with my sister-in-law and had just sat down. The waitress came out and said, 'Cindy Perino, there's a call for you.' It was my father-in-law. He said there had been a shooting at Columbine, and they didn't know anything about Frank yet. I'll never forget the look on Cindy's face when she came back to the table.*

"I got up right away because I wanted to find my mom and dad and Tony and get down to the school. I remember the bartender was crying; he was a former student of Frank's. When I found my mom, she told me she had heard about the shooting because someone from Entertainment Tonight *had called her.* "

Anthony DeAngelis

" *I was working at my shop, The Hair Team, and a client came in and said, 'Hey, did you hear about the shooting at Columbine?' I hadn't, but then the phone calls started coming in. We didn't have the smartphones and social media we have now. I tried to call Frank. There was a personal phone number he would always answer. It rang and rang. I said, 'Okay, this is not good.' I left a message thinking he would call me back, but he didn't. More and more people came in asking, 'Did you hear?' and I said, 'We're finding out.' My clients encouraged me to leave the shop to find out more. I thought I might be able to get to the school because one of my clients, Dave Hendrickson, was a district administrator, and I knew he'd be there.* "

Later, we learned that the gunmen first killed students Rachel Scott and Daniel Rohrbough and wounded others outside. School resource officer Neil Gardner, a deputy in the Jeffco Sheriff's Department, was returning to campus from lunch and had entered the parking lot in an unmarked patrol vehicle. Harris fired multiple shots in Gardner's direction with an assault rifle. Gardner returned fire with a .45-caliber semi-automatic pistol. Klebold and Harris then rushed into the building and headed toward the library. Following protocol, Gardner stayed outside.

Wounded in the hallway, Dave Sanders crawled until another teacher saw him and dragged him into Science Room 3, where some students were hiding.

The killers entered the library and went on a murderous rampage. In only seven minutes, from 11:29 to 11:36, they fatally wounded ten and shot and injured twelve more.

That's the short version.

My purpose here is not to replay the horrors, but to give you the context of the timetable and strategy.

The first SWAT team finally entered the east doors at 12:06 p.m., forty-seven minutes after the first shots were fired and a half-hour after Harris and Klebold had left the library following their killing spree.

They wandered the hallways for a bit, looking at students through glass in locked doors but not trying to shoot or force their way in. They returned to the cafeteria twice in efforts to check on and try to get their propane bombs to explode, then they tossed bombs into the hallways. The killers then returned to the library at 12:08 and shot themselves. At that point, they had not added to the death toll for half an hour.

When the killers died, the first police—the SWAT officers— had been in the building for two minutes.

Today, that strategy of waiting seems nuts. But it was the protocol of the time.

One of my dear friends, AJ DeAndrea, was part of the first and second SWAT team sweeps of the building, and he and others were angry about the delays.

As we waited outside, we didn't know much about what was going on. Cell phone service was spotty back then, but a student and some teachers had called out and were sharing information with us. The kid told his father that there were about sixty students in the vocal music room. Then all of a sudden, we heard more gunfire. We assumed the gunmen were still shooting, but we later learned that round of fire was the SWAT team, shooting its way into the building.

A second SWAT team went through the windows of the teachers' lounge on the west side of the school at 1:09 p.m.

The two killers had been dead for sixty-one minutes.

Patrick Ireland, a junior shot twice in the head by Klebold in the library, managed to complete his agonizing crawl across the library floor and climb out the second-floor window into the arms of two SWAT officers at 2:38. After that, he became known as "The Boy in the Window."

The two killers had been dead for two hours and thirty minutes.

But we didn't know that.

SWAT officers didn't reach Dave Sanders in Science Room 3 until 2:40, and after they radioed for help, a Denver paramedic arrived about 3:10 and pronounced Dave dead. Shot in the carotid artery, Dave bled to death, despite heroic efforts of students to keep him alive.

Officers didn't get to the library and find the bodies of the killers and the students murdered there until 3:22.

The school wasn't declared secure until 4:00. By then, the killers had been dead for nearly four hours.

With all the police blockades set up around Columbine, my brother, Anthony, hadn't been able to reach the school. Instead, he went to Leawood Elementary, where students were being brought by buses to meet their parents.

Anthony DeAngelis

> ❝ I ran into Dave Hendrickson at Leawood. He said, 'Come into this room; let me tell you what's going on. Right now, your brother's up at the command post. I'll take you there. You need to be with him.' But before we could leave, he came back and said, 'No, we're bringing Frank here.' ❞

There were so many rumors. People threw numbers around, and it was hard to sort through what was real and what was speculation. That uncertainty continued for many hours—even days. The next morning's *Denver Post,* with a late-night deadline, reported that the death toll was "as many as twenty-five people." The rival *Rocky Mountain News* ran a picture taken from a helicopter overhead, showing a murdered and as-yet unidentified Daniel Rohrbough next to a pool of blood outside the building. The decision to run that image is one I know newspaper editors regretted, but it was 1999, a time when the internet was young and print news still pre-eminent.

When the first SWAT team members came out, I knew some of them, and they said, "Frank, it's bad."

I went to Leawood at around 7 p.m. and found my brother, Anthony, waiting for me, as were Cheryl and my childhood friend John Wasinger. Anthony didn't leave my side for the rest of the night.

Anthony DeAngelis

> *The rest of the night, it was him and me. Frank said, 'I have to get into the school, I have to get into the school.' I said, 'Frank, we can't.' We talked, and he was trying to explain what had happened. It felt like a movie. I hate to say this, but it was like you were waiting for Stallone to come busting through and save everyone. That's what it seemed like. I kept thinking, This isn't happening.*

As buses arrived and unloaded at Leawood, Assistant Principal Kevin Land called out the names of the students, and parents came up and got their kids. He had the rosters of kids so we could try to account for the students. I saw wave after wave of emotional reunions and tears of relief. As the night went on, fewer people got off the buses. By about 9:30, parents were coming up and asking me if I had seen their sons or daughters. I couldn't give them the answers they wanted. I held onto the hope that some of the kids had walked home or found rides with friends, but I knew there was a good chance some of the waiting parents would get horrible news soon.

Finally, there were no more buses. All the kids were out of the building except for those who had lost their lives. The grief counselor came and asked me to join him as he told the parents. They were gathered into a room, and they were told their children might have died. The anguish of that moment and the looks of despair on their faces will remain with me for the rest of my life. There simply are no words of comfort for that kind of grief.

Adding to my own grief that evening was the loss of my friend, Dave Sanders. One of the rumors that day had been that a teacher with a beard had been shot and had been transported to the hospital. By this time, I knew that Dave had been killed and found by the

SWAT team earlier in the day. But when I saw technology teacher Rich Long, who had been with Dave and saw Dave's blood on his shirt . . . that got to me. Days later, I listened to the voicemail messages left by Dave's wife, Linda, and his daughters from that day, asking for him to call them to let them know he was okay. I still get emotional whenever I think about those voicemail messages.

With everyone accounted for, it was finally time to go home. The police didn't want me to stay at my house that night, because they were concerned for my safety. When we left Leawood, Anthony drove, avoiding the media reporters who had been camped around the school all evening. We stopped by my house for clothes and were surprised that there were no media vans waiting for us. While I gathered a few things, Anthony went by my neighbor's house and asked him to keep an eye on my home and to call us at Anthony's if there was any trouble. From there, we went to Anthony and Shanda's house, where Cheryl, Hayley, and my parents met us. I can remember arriving at the house and just feeling numb. I was in shock and filled with feelings of guilt. No one seemed to know what to say, although my family kept telling me it was not my fault.

The phone calls started coming from the media. They knew Anthony was my brother, and they assumed I was there, or that Anthony knew where I was. He asked them to wait until the morning.

Stunned and angry, I mourned the dead. I knew that my life—and the lives of those affected—never would be the same. That day, we grieved as the world witnessed our vulnerability. Evil had devalued precious human lives and ripped away at peace. The tragedy of that day changed our community—and our country—forever.

Chapter Six

Aftermath

What little sleep I got that night was fitful. Early the next morning, Kevin Land picked me for a 6:00 a.m. meeting with the School Board President, Jon DeStefano, and Superintendent Jane Hammond at the Jefferson County education building. My car still was in the school faculty lot and police weren't allowing any of the vehicles to be moved until they were checked for bombs.

I told Jon I would do whatever I had to do to help in the recovery and healing. If that meant resigning, I would do so on the spot.

"You're not going anywhere," Jon said. His words meant so much to me. I knew that he was facing difficult decisions and pressure to pinpoint blame, so his support encouraged me as we started our road to recovery.

That morning, students, parents, and faculty members, along with school district and government officials, all gathered at Light of the World Catholic Church to grieve together and to honor those we had lost. We were all stunned and hurting. We hadn't awakened and discovered it was only a bad dream.

We were facing the unknown. There were no manuals for how to handle what would come next.

Representatives from the school district, law enforcement, and faith community spoke first, trying to reassure our community that we would heal together. But the kids didn't know them.

They knew me. I knew they needed to hear from me—and I knew I needed to speak to them. I tried to jot down some things I wanted to say before it was my turn to speak, but I couldn't find the words. Then someone announced my name. As I stood, the students and others, many of them who previously had shown little emotion, started crying. They stood and began clapping. They roared in an expression of solidarity and support—for each other and for me. These kids knew that some people were looking for someone to blame other than the killers and their parents, and they knew that, at times, that someone was going to be me.

Their support in that moment weighed heavily against the guilt I felt. Overcome with emotion, I turned away from the crowd and sobbed uncontrollably, until I was finally able to gather myself and start speaking. "I am so sorry for what happened and what you are feeling," I said. "I'd like to take a wand and wipe away what you are feeling, but I can't do that. I'd like to tell you these scars will heal, but they will not."

That was when I promised the students I would stay at Columbine through at least the spring of 2002, when the current freshmen would graduate. Our journey to recovery had begun, and we were going to be in it together. I told them I loved them, just as I had done the previous Friday at the prom assembly

Feeling supported, individually and as a community, was an essential part of our healing. For me, that meant taking advice from John Fisher, the chiropractor my mother worked for at the time. John was a Vietnam War veteran. He had not gone through therapy to learn how to cope with the flashbacks and trauma related to his military service until after they had taken a considerable toll. He called me that day and said, "Frank, you're going to find every reason to help others but not help yourself. But if you don't help yourself, you're not going to be able to help anybody else."

Earlier that day a district official had told me that if I sought counseling, I probably shouldn't tell anyone; it would be considered a sign of weakness. The implication was that I would lose my job because I would be deemed unfit for duty.

The comment made by that district official still disturbs me. Counseling was a critical part of my own recovery, and what I gained from it put me in a better state to support and help others. I feel so strongly about the benefits of counseling after a tragic event that I recently joined Kiki Leyba's wife, Kallie Leyba, to address the Douglas County School Board in Colorado to encourage them to put a policy in place that requires counseling for all educators after a horrific event, just as first responders receive. That's not common practice for educators across the nation.

Kallie, a member of the American Federation of Teachers, worked to pass a resolution for post-traumatic care for educators at the AFT 2018 Convention. The nation's second largest teachers' union is resolved to push for mandatory mental health support for teachers and staff across the country as we continue to cope with mass shootings in our schools.

Our staff members returned to work two weeks after the tragedy. I wish now that each staff member had talked to a mental health worker to make sure they had the support they needed to return to the classroom to teach and counsel the students.

Thankfully, I listened to John and found a therapist, Patrick Maloney. The help he has given me through the years since has been invaluable. District employee Betsy Thompson also was supportive of me and our school community. Dr. John Nicoletti did counseling work for the school district, and the advice he offered me and staff members at Columbine was crucial to our recovery. Seeking help also meant leaning on my friends. Rick DeBell, as always, stood by me. His support was a great help during the next few months . . . and beyond.

Rick DeBell

66 *My wife and I and my family tried to help as much as we could, without reliving it and bringing back the thoughts of that day. We always tried to be a little bit more on the positive side of things. To this day, we don't talk about it much unless Frank mentions it. But Columbine is his family, was his family. To this day, I know that's where his heart is, that's where his life is, that's why he always will carry on—because that's his family.* 99

Even as the shock and grief numbed us, school board members, district leaders, law enforcement officers, and my administrative team had to make decisions about the Columbine student body's immediate future. The assistant principals and I met with district leaders, including Jon DeStefano and Jane Hammond, to talk about when and where to resume classes. We knew it couldn't be in the Columbine building. We also decided that skipping the rest of the school year wasn't an option. That would be giving in. There was some discussion about dividing up the student body, spreading them out among the other schools in the south Jeffco area. The principals at those schools—Dakota Ridge, Chatfield, and Bear Creek—all reached out with offers, but I felt strongly that we needed to be together.

Eventually, we decided to resume classes after the thirteen memorial services had concluded. We would do it as a full student body at Chatfield, sharing the building in two shifts. Chatfield's classes would be held in the morning and ours in the afternoon. Chatfield principal Sally Blanchard (who had been the Columbine athletic director when I was coaching) and the rest of her school opened their doors to us. More importantly, they opened their hearts to us. Barb Monseu, my supervisor, and Dr. Cindy Stevenson were instrumental in supporting the decision and remained my strongest advocates as we moved forward.

West Bowles Community Church became our school's *de facto* meeting place for a short time. It was a central location for faculty members to meet each day and for the kids to gather and support one another and to talk with counselors. I went there April 22, but chose to stay in an office outside the auditorium. I still felt numb and hadn't been eating or sleeping, so at that moment I had nothing to give. As I prayed, hoping to find answers, I deferred to other adults to meet with the students until a counselor came and got me, saying, "The kids want you." When I entered the auditorium, the students called out, "We love you, Mr. De!" and "We are Columbine."

I lost it again. Their love and support for me brought a fresh wave of tears to my eyes. I couldn't speak through the emotion that choked my voice. I walked down from the stage and embraced my students as I walked through the auditorium.

A counselor later told me, "Frank, even though you didn't say a word, your actions spoke louder than any message you could have delivered because you gave those kids permission to cry."

At that point, the counselors were worried about the guys who showed no emotion. When I started crying, many of the kids started shedding tears right along with me. Guys who had been stoic for two days started crying too.

That night there were more tears at the community candle-light prayer vigil at St. Frances Cabrini Catholic Church. I initially balked when Father Ken Leone called and asked me to come to the church that night. I had been a part of that parish since moving out to the area in 1980. I was an usher at Sunday Masses, and I was part of the youth programs, so I felt a strong connection to that church. But that night, I was reluctant to go.

"Frank, you need to come down," he said.

"Father, I have so much going on . . . " I started.

"No," Father Leone declared. "You need to come down to the church."

At that point, I was asking myself the question so many were wondering: "How could God—my God—let this happen?" I had stayed awake at my brother's home that night, asking that question. I was a "Cradle Catholic," and I never remember questioning my faith to the extent I did at that point.

Through the anger and the pain, I wanted to know that answer. The meeting at the church was where my healing began.

Father Leone, without revealing the details of what was planned, wouldn't take no for an answer. When I walked in, there must have been twelve hundred people in the church, and many of them were Columbine kids who were part of the church's youth program. I remember making eye contact with Tom Tonelli there. His presence comforted me.

Tom Tonelli

66 Our hearts just poured out to him. I think the people who know and love De felt that way. I just looked him in the eye. I said, 'Frank, if there's anything you need . . .' Remembering that moment still brings me to tears.

"I think a lot of us thought that the only way we were going to get through everything was if God carried us through it. You're devastated on so many levels. It's not private. It's national. It's already a sensational story that's being further sensationalized in the media. Of course, I don't want to compare anything

I (or we) had to go through to anything those families had to go through. The loss that they still must feel is so much more painful, so far beyond my comprehension. 🙶

Father Leone called me to the altar in the center of the sanctuary and asked the students in attendance to lay their hands on me as he prayed. He whispered in my ear: "Frank, you were spared for a reason. You should have died. God has a plan for you. Now you need to rebuild that community."

He could tell I was feeling the weight of the world on my shoulders, so he added, "You're not going to have to walk this journey alone."

I had grown up in the Church, and his words reminded me why faith was so important. That night, Father Leone told me, "Frank, I have no answers. How could this happen in our community? But we have to live by faith and not by sight." He went on to say, "In his heart, a man plans his course, but the Lord determines his steps." That's from Proverbs 16:9.

That night, Father Leone's words marked a turning point for me. I became even more determined to continue and try to be at the forefront of the recovery. I was truly blessed to have the ongoing support of the spiritual leadership at St. Frances Cabrini from Father Leone, Father Michael Pavlakovich, Father Sean McGrath, Father Nathan Goebel, Deacon Chet Ubowski, and Youth Group Minster Jim Beckman. From St. Mark, Father Kenneth Koehler provided support. I was honored at the Chatfield-Columbine football game, and Father Sean attended it with my family. Father Sean and my dad were both from Montclair, New Jersey, and they shared stories. From Mount Carmel, Father Mark Franceschini and Father Hugh Guentner were there for me. The Mount Carmel Men's Club offered support, and that has been a constant ever since. All the area churches came together for the kids and the community; faith was something everyone needed during those dark days. The churches opened their doors and their hearts. Even for people who didn't have that faith and that background or who weren't believers, it helped. When I retired and moved to Arvada, I continued to serve as an usher at St. Frances Cabrini every other month. I was truly blessed that Father Sean McGrath became pastor at St. Anne's and Father Nathan Goebel at St. Joan of Arc. Both parishes are in Arvada and have welcomed Diane and me with open arms and provide a spiritual home for us. Attendance at daily Mass continues to provide the strength that I need during my retirement.

Kiki Leyba

> " Frank was still in a state of shock, but he felt the need to take care of the school community. I think everybody still was at a loss, wondering what healing looked like. In that moment, everybody was fumbling through it—law enforcement, district officials, our administrative team. People had pieces of information, but there still was a lot that was unknown. There was no handbook about what we would do next. "

I didn't speak to any media until Friday. District officials said I needed to respond, so I agreed to talk with Katie Couric from NBC's *Today*. The media had set up a broadcasting command post in Clement Park. As Couric and I sat in the dark at about 5 a.m. on Friday, I saw the yellow crime tape around Columbine and kept thinking back to how beautiful that Tuesday morning had been. And now it was cold and snowing. There in the darkness, I wondered if our community would ever see those bright skies again at Columbine. But I had to believe. If I was going to fulfill what

Father Leone asked me to do, I needed to lead as we started on the road to recovery. I needed to take to heart the message from John 8:12: "When Jesus spoke again to the people, he said, 'I am the light of the world. Whoever follows me will never walk in darkness but will have the light of life.'" After the interview, I realized even more that every move we made was—and to an extent, would continue to be—under the microscope. I prayed that the darkness on that early Friday morning would give way to light for our community.

In the days that followed the shooting, we learned more about what had happened, and we grieved in the national spotlight. Governor Bill Owens went to the school to see the devastation for himself. At that point, I felt I needed to go back into that building, too. I contacted authorities, and on that Saturday after the tragedy, FBI agent Dwayne Fuselier, whose kids had gone to Columbine, escorted me into my school.

I had walked through those doors every school day for almost twenty years—as a teacher, coach, and principal—but that day, I didn't know what to expect when I walked in. I went by my office and saw the damage the killers had done to the office and various areas in the hallway. That was a big deal at that point because of the talk that the killers were targeting jocks. But there were things in that building that represented the athletic program. There was a hanging trophy case, and if you really wanted to make a statement about the culture, the first thing you would do is shoot up the trophy case. Peter Horvath, one of the deans of students, had been a successful soccer coach, and his office was across from mine. His whole office was soccer memorabilia and pictures and programs. They did nothing to his office. Again, if they were going after a "jock culture" they could have easily damaged Mr. Horvath's office.

From my office, we walked down the hallway.

We could see knuckle prints in blood embedded in the carpet near the library where Dave Sanders had been fatally wounded.

Seeing the blood on the carpet where my friend had tried to crawl to safety got to me more than anything else that day.

I wasn't allowed to enter the library that day. It was a mess and considered a crime scene, with the police still collecting evidence. (My return to the library came later.) But I did go into the science room where the kids had tried to help Dave before the paramedics moved him to another room, where he eventually died. When I saw the outline of his body and the bloodstained sweatshirts that the kids had used to try to stop the bleeding and keep him alive, I broke down and wept uncontrollably. Many of the police officers and agents I had dealt with, even the ones I knew, had this professional demeanor. They were "tough." But Dwayne grabbed me and held me as I sobbed.

When I'd pulled myself together again, we walked down the stairs to the cafeteria. Seeing the standing water caused by the fire-alarm system having been set off, all I could think about was what it was like for those kids and staff members as they ran to save their lives. The memories always will be etched on my mind.

That day, the tremendous support I felt from friends and loved ones helped carry me through. My parents, siblings, and extended family: Tony's wife, Shanda; LuAnn's husband, Ted Dwyer; my nephews and nieces Teddy and Sabrina Dwyer and Michael and Laura Askins—had always been there with me during the good, and they stood by me throughout this nightmare.

Chapter Seven

The Thirteen

Iknew some of the murdered students a little better than others, but they were all "my" kids, and I felt each of their losses personally. At each of the thirteen memorial services, we grieved the stolen years and the lives of promise left unfulfilled.

Junior Cassie Bernall wanted to be an obstetrician.

Freshman Steven Curnow could recite entire speeches from *Star Wars* and loved soccer.

Junior Corey DePooter worked at Raccoon Creek Golf Course and that week planned to pick up the Mustang he had bought with his earnings.

Sophomore Kelly Fleming hoped to be a writer and songwriter.

Sophomore Matt Kechter was a straight-A student and seemed destined to be a starting football lineman in ensuing years.

Sophomore Daniel Mauser was the top biology student in the sophomore class and was a member of the Speech and Debate team.

Freshman Daniel Rohrbough was a stereo expert who worked on his grandfather's farm in Kansas during the summers.

Junior Rachel Scott was active in theater and drama, was writing a play, and was on the Speech and Debate team.

Senior Isaiah Shoels decided not to play football, as he realized his keyboard talents would be more appropriate for the music world.

Sophomore John Tomlin loved his Chevy truck and helped build a house for a poor family in Mexico while serving in a Missions Ministries project.

Senior Lauren Townsend was a star in both volleyball and the classroom. She maintained a perfect 4.0 GPA and was anxious to head out into the world to save the planet and animals she so dearly loved.

Sophomore Kyle Velasquez had suffered a stroke as a young boy and fought through it, earning the respect and affection of his classmates.

Dave Sanders was the model teacher-coach. Especially because of our discussion at the baseball game the day before his death, and because of his actions in running into the hallway, I still feel survivor's guilt when I think of Dave.

The first memorial service was for Rachel Scott, on Saturday, April 24, and the others took place the next week. On the day after Rachel's service, a public gathering was held at Southwest Plaza, the nearby mall where the students often went for lunch at the food court. Senior Amber Burgess sang the national anthem and then delivered an emotional speech. Vice President Al Gore also spoke at that service. I was amazed by the courage exhibited by our students as they spoke publicly after the tragedy. Once again, our grief was publicized for the world to see.

Each memorial service reopened our wounds. Every time we honored the lives that were ended far too soon, we thought about what might have been. At the same time, the services and community gatherings gave us a time and space to work through the five stages of grief—denial, anger, bargaining, depression and, finally, acceptance. As a community, we tried to come up with answers. Personally, I felt angry and depressed. I wanted to remain isolated, but it was impossible because of all the public events I attended. Whenever I had the chance, I wanted to be alone. My family and friends had difficulty understanding my state of mind. I was grateful for their love and support, but I was experiencing survivor's guilt, and I did not want to relive the events. I had a difficult time looking at people in the eyes because of the guilt I felt.

That first weekend, I tried to visit all the families who had lost a child. Some district officials advised me not to make those visits because they were concerned that some of the families might consider or take legal action against me and/or the district. I understood the concern, but I told them I didn't care how it would affect my job; it was the right thing to do.

I didn't get a chance to talk to the Rohrboughs, but I did talk to Sue and Rich Petrone, Danny Rohrbough's mom and stepfather. Nicole Petrone, Danny's stepsister, was one of the girls with me as we fled from the gunman and hid in the gymnasium.

At every turn, I was being told what to do, what to say, and whom to talk to. It seemed as if every move I made was under the world's microscope. I remember an anonymous quote: *In our lives, sometimes we have to stand up for what is right even though we are standing alone.* I heeded that advice to the chagrin of some of the people advising me.

Finding the right words to say to those families was tough. What do you say? Sometimes just being there and offering support helped, but every visit was difficult. Three weeks later, around Mother's Day, I visited the mothers and took them flowers.

When the staff met at the West Bowles church, I looked around at my administrative team. I knew we would be tested. I took roll call with my eyes and my heart. Kevin Land, Karen Studenka,

Maria Reschke, Peter Horvath, and Chris Mikesell were my fellow administrators. (Pat Patrick would join our team the following year and was a great support for me.) Judy Asbury, Brad Butts, Ryan Collins, Joe Cunningham, Ken Holden, and Susan Peters formed the counseling staff. Susan White was my secretary and educational assistant. (Later, Karen Jones would replace Susan.) We were a team swimming in uncharted waters and each day was a learning experience.

We committed to be there for one another for what we realized would be a marathon, not a sprint. And we stood by one another—for years.

The fact that we only had about three weeks left in the school year made resuming classes a little more manageable. During the healing process, the members of the Columbine school community had the support of the principals and their staffs from our rival high schools. Jim Ellis, Keith Mead, and Wendy Rubin from Chatfield, and Tim MacDonnell and Jim Jelinek from Dakota Ridge all helped. Feeder schools in the Columbine attendance area also were affected by the tragedy. Principals Dr. Armistead Webster of Columbine Hills Elementary, Peggy Taylor of Dutch Creek Elementary, LuAnn Schwartz of Governors Ranch Elementary, Dr. Cindy Partridge of Leawood Elementary, Cynthia Hawes of Normandy Elementary, and George Diedrich of Ken Caryl Middle School were also supportive. Columbine's spirit involved more than one school.

I continued to examine and even question my faith during the recovery, but ultimately it was strengthened. I remembered a Bible verse, 2 Corinthians 5:7, "For we walk by faith, not by sight," and that helped alleviate my doubts. Over the years, I had priests, one right after the other, there to help me. And I had my family and friends. Especially initially after the tragedy, I was struggling to work through my own grief and recovery. But I couldn't let that derail me from the mission at hand—the Columbine recovery.

LuAnn DeAngelis Dwyer

" *Frank was in shock much of the time, but I think that's where his faith helped tremendously. He was not going to let this beat him, no matter what. When we went to our dinners, he didn't want to talk about it much. But when he did, that's when we knew we needed to listen.* "

Anthony DeAngelis

" *He would call me, and I knew I would have to drop what I was doing to talk. His friends would call, and they were concerned, and it's not that he wanted to blow them off; he just couldn't talk to them. That was the big thing. So when he called, I knew he had to get something off his chest. I was glad I could be there to help him with that part of it.* "

There's a saying that when someone you love becomes a memory, the memory becomes a treasure. I have found that to be true. Each morning, I recited the names of those we had lost. As long as I'm alive, I will continue sharing their names and telling their stories. Not a day passes that I don't think of the Beloved Thirteen.

Chapter Eight

The Killers

It saddens me that while the killers' names are mentioned often, those of the murder victims are not, which is why I keep thinking I might cut this chapter before you have a chance to read it. If it remains, know that I included it with great reluctance. Much—*too much*—has been written about the killers.

They desired attention, even in death. They succeeded in attaining it. In fact, years later, many in the media still are preoccupied with the killers and their warped motives.

And along with all the morbid curiosity, there are voices of accusation: *Columbine's leaders should have known. Columbine's leaders should have seen it coming.*

We all wish the killers' plot had been discovered and derailed. But the idea that anyone should have suspected the merciless attack is naïve and mostly misguided. If the early reporting, which led people to believe these kids walked around the school hallways all but announcing their plans, had been accurate, then yes, we would have been negligent in our responsibility to protect our students and staff members.

But the reality of what happened is so much more complicated than that.

Klebold and Harris were a couple of intelligent kids who could turn on the charm when they needed to and come off as, at worst, the troublesome kids next door.

They were far more evil than that.

They stored up hate. They plotted. They assembled arsenals.

In January of that year, Klebold turned in violent writings in a creative writing class. They weren't so extraordinary that we considered them as potential foreshadowing, but neither were they ignored. The teacher, Judy Kelly, expressed her concern, and spoke to Klebold, his parents, and counselor Brad Butts. Klebold was convincing when he explained that it was just a story for a creative writing class. Of course, if we'd known more about the killers' actions as they continued their plotting, the writing might have raised more red flags.

But we didn't have more information at the time. Their plotting took place outside of school, usually in the Harris basement. That's where they chronicled their plan for more than a year in what came to be known as "The Basement Tapes."

Media reports painted a picture that the killers were kids "on the outside" at Columbine. Wrong. What we saw were two kids in advanced placement classes. Klebold was in the gifted and talented program throughout elementary school. Harris took steps, however insincere, to join the Marines, but the fact that he was taking the prescription antidepressant Luvox kept him from being accepted by the Corps.

Much later, it became known that in 1998, Jefferson County Sheriff's Office Investigator Mike Guerra looked at Harris' website and wrote a draft affidavit for a search warrant of his home after he had threatened a fellow student. The parents of that student had reported the threat to the Sheriff's office, but the search warrant never was filed. Neither Harris' threat toward the other student nor the drafted affidavit were brought to our attention at the school, at least not until after Harris and Klebold attacked.

The misinformation from the media also included ridiculous reports about the "Trench Coat Mafia." That group, whose members wore black trench coats, was small and considered harmless. They liked to play Dungeons and Dragons and appeared together in an unalarming yearbook picture in 1998. While Klebold and Harris sometimes wore trench coats, they weren't in that picture, and they were never considered part of the group. In fact, by 1999, most of the members of the Trench Coat Mafia had graduated. Yes, the killers wore trench coats as they headed into the school that day, but it wasn't to advertise a group affiliation; it was to hide their weapons.

In late 1999, along with the families of the dead and wounded, I viewed The Basement Tapes at the Jefferson County Sheriff's office. What we saw sickened us all. That's when I realized how evil these kids really had been. Hearing the chilling hatred in Harris' heart, we learned that he idolized Adolf Hitler; he quoted Hitler's anti-Semitic book *Mein Kampf*—My Struggle. He talked about survival of the fittest and killing the weak. His diatribe was evil and frightening and made it clear to all of us that he was a psychopath who felt no remorse for his intent to kill as many people as possible.

The reasons for their hatred were both simple and irrational. The way a kid laughed or said "expresso" instead of "espresso" was enough to earn the loathing of the killers. Although neither of the boys bullied other kids physically, it was clear they disdained those whom they saw as beneath them.

Susan Klebold, Dylan Klebold's mother, wrote in her book, published in 2016, that she originally thought Dylan had been brainwashed by Harris. She recognized that Harris bullied Klebold mentally and emotionally even though Klebold was bigger physically. When she saw The Basement Tapes, however, she realized that her son was just as violent as Harris. In her book and public talks, Ms. Klebold says she believes Dylan was in a state of depression his senior year but that she'd had no idea he was capable of murder. She had feared he was suicidal. Her greatest regret is that she didn't get him the help he needed.

Unfortunately, after limited viewings, the tapes were ordered sealed and then destroyed. I understand the fear that, if they were public record, they would be tools for imitators and copycats. But I wish psychologists and other professionals could have viewed the tapes. As disturbing as they were, the recordings contained lessons about the killers that could potentially prevent future attacks by others.

The killers kept their evil, along with the arsenal of weapons and materials for bombs, well hidden. They were intentional about maintaining their front, but they seemed prideful about their planning, noting on the tapes that it was too bad nobody would see the tapes until it was too late.

During the investigation, I had to keep my mouth shut about what was on the tapes. Those who viewed the tapes were under a gag order about some aspects of the attack and the events leading up to it, including the details of what was on those recordings. But I said over and over that the truth would come out.

The tapes and other police documentation raised questions about the killers' parents and their lack of monitoring as their children put together their disgusting plans. I *wish* the parents of the two killers would have taken some action. When the police arrived at the Harris house, the parents admitted that no one ever went into his room. If they had gone into his room, they would have found pipe bombs. Even when the evidence was in their faces, they seemed to ignore it. In late 1998, a gun store clerk called the Harris home and said an ammunition order had arrived. With Eric in earshot, Mr. Harris replied that he hadn't ordered anything. In reality, Eric had ordered nine ten-round magazines for one of their rifles. Because he had pre-paid for them, he brazenly walked into the gun store and picked up the ammunition, no questions asked. In his journal, Harris counted the incident as among the number of times they were almost caught.

And, if Harris' parents had walked into the basement, we wouldn't be talking about Columbine in the way we do today. In his rambling manifestos, Harris left behind more evidence than Klebold did of his intentions. Klebold wiped clean his computer hard drive. But it is wrong to say Klebold was a passive Harris follower. They were partners in their plan to terrorize and murder their classmates. The question that cannot be answered is, would they have carried out their act of terrorism individually?

It angers me that multiple myths about Columbine stubbornly remain and are often repeated as truth. One falsehood was that that there was widespread and extraordinary "bullying" at Columbine and that athletes mistreated the two killers in a school where a "jock culture" ruled. We had one of Colorado's most successful football programs, yet the bullying charge was not only ridiculously exaggerated, it was also repeatedly expressed by people who failed to evaluate the situation in the context of the universal high school experience. Sure, isolated bullying occurred at Columbine; it occurs in all high schools. Sorry, it does. Sadly, it does. When I went to Mount Carmel Junior High, a Catholic school with nuns and priests, there was bullying going on. That said, the killers were *not* bullied into a path where murder was their only escape.

Kiki Leyba

❝ *Should Frank have known that this might happen? There's no way. No way. He didn't have anything to tell him, not a rumor, not a 1 percent chance. He didn't have anything. Other people had little pieces, but Frank didn't. When the school took such a beating in the media about the climate of the school and the jock culture and bullying, it was wrong. After doing my student teaching at Columbine, I knew it was a place I wanted to work. I remember telling friends, 'This place is amazing! It's something special. It's not like other schools. There's a close-knit culture; it's a real family vibe.' It was cool to be smart, it was cool to be high performing, it was cool to be involved. It was a place of belonging. It was a place of close-ness. You could float between groups of kids who might have been self-labeled as skaters or jocks, but there weren't these hard lines. It was a place where you could have your identity, but you didn't feel like you had to hang only with your own people. You could see the positive culture and acceptance. It was palpable. So to hear that talk about bullying in the media was really difficult, and I knew that was hard for Frank, too, to hear what people said about his school and the climate he was so much a part of creating. His legacy is creating that feeling of tradition and family.* ❞

The bullying myths were, and continue to be, perpetuated by media. In 2016, I saw the movie about Rachel Scott, *I'm Not Ashamed*. In it, the Columbine athletes are portrayed as big bruis-ers walking around in white T-shirts and white hats. One scene has the athletes drenching Harris in baby oil in the hallway and then picking him up and sliding him down the hallway. They called it *bowling*. I grew more and more angry as I watched the ridiculous scene in which adults stood by watching the abuse. I know my staff, and I would bet everything we own on the fact that if adults at Columbine saw something like that, they would stop it from happening. Plus, before the tragedy, there was carpeting throughout the building. The moviemakers had this kid sliding on a smooth, uncovered floor.

I called the people who made the movie and they cited "dramatic license."

I said, "This is a pretty significant thing because people are saying, 'How could staff members just watch this happen?'"

Well, they didn't. It didn't happen.

I'm not saying bullying never happened at Columbine, but we did everything we could to discourage bullying and create a culture in which it was rare. I know, without a doubt, that bullying was not the cause of the murderous attacks. Even Susan Klebold agrees that bullying wasn't the reason her son and Harris carried out their plan. In her book she notes that her son never mentioned bullying in his journal entries. Bullying was not mentioned in Harris's journal entries either.

Shortly after the tragedy, a reporter contacted me wanting to confirm a story about the two killers being sprayed by other kids with ketchup and mustard in the cafeteria. Supposedly, the teachers in the cafeteria were standing up and cheering as they watched the scene. Then the boys reportedly came to me and said it was embarrassing; they didn't want me to do anything, but they wanted to go home and change their clothes before their next classes. The ridiculous narrative was that I told them they were losers who deserved that treatment, and they had to go straight to class.

How absurd! But that was the kind of garbage floating around. At least this time, the reporter contacted me to verify the story. Of course, I told the reporter that none of that ever happened.

The next day, the headline read, "DeAngelis Denies Bullying Ever Took Place."

Fiction was repeatedly reported as fact. Inaccurate and shoddily researched stories circulated in the media. Adding to the problem was the reality that anyone with a computer and the internet could claim to be a "journalist" and write whatever they dreamed up. I learned that if someone had a slant on the story and believed in it strongly, they would interview a thousand people until they found one who would give them the story they wanted. I would be naïve to think that all two thousand kids at Columbine were going to be happy at the high school. But some of the stuff in some of the media was just bizarre.

LuAnn DeAngelis Dwyer

66 *Everybody was saying, 'We understand; that's your brother.' I said, 'Yeah, he's my brother, but I also know what kind of person he is. I know his heart. You don't get it.'* 99

Anthony DeAngelis

66 *I told Frank, 'Let me be your spokesman. I will go kick the shit out of them.' He said, 'No, one day it will all come out.' It was so tough to see how beat up he was getting on a daily basis. We knew what they were saying was not what he was about.* 99

With all the stories that were told, most missed the scariest point: The carnage could have been much more devastating if the murderers' two homemade bombs had gone off as planned. Hidden in the duffle bags that Harris and Klebold placed in the cafeteria before going back outside, the bombs were set to go off during the early minutes of the lunch period. Had the bombs worked, the second-floor library would have fallen in on the first-floor cafeteria while it was full of students. The killers waited outside, planning to shoot students as they tried to escape the devastation. If their plan had worked, my horrifying guess is that seven hundred students and staff members could have died that day. In addition, they had bombs in their cars, strategically placed where first responders would arrive. The bombs in their cars did not explode.

The killers wanted to kill, plain and simple. Reports kept coming out that they had targeted athletes, Christians, or black students, but that is inaccurate. By placing bombs in the cafeteria, they weren't targeting anyone; they were targeting *everyone*. If they were targeting athletes, they could have easily walked into the weight room. They had a "hit list," but paid no attention to it. No one on the hit list was shot. Their actions weren't reprisal for supposed bullying. The intent was to blow up the school and take as many students with them as possible. It was vicious, virulent, disgusting, indiscriminate hatred in action.

As I've noted, ten died and twelve were wounded in the library. The Jefferson County Sheriff's report later said a total of fifty-two students and four adults were in the library when the killers entered the first time. They had enough ammunition to kill all fifty-six. For seven minutes, they taunted and fired. At that point, the selectivity gave them power as they decided who would die and who would live.

In late 1999, the FBI put together a panel from various schools where shootings had occurred. Everybody seemed to have an answer to the question of how to prevent a school massacre from ever happening again. A profiler went through a checklist of risk factors to watch for. When he was done, a principal at the meeting stood up and said, "Well, I've got a school of about 1,500. Right now, according to your checklist, I have about 800 kids that are potential killers."

Yes, it seems so easy.

Even before I saw The Basement Tapes, the FBI showed me a letter that Harris had written to the people who owned a van that he and Klebold had burglarized in January 1998. The letter was so apologetic. He told those people he was so sorry he had violated their personal property, he knew the burglary victims probably wouldn't be able to forgive, but he said he wasn't a bad kid and he had let down his parents.

Then the same FBI agent showed me parts of their journals that were laden with "f-bombs" and noted that people deserved to die.

They'd had people fooled.

Not long before April 20, 1999, Klebold went down to the University of Arizona with his parents. He had just been accepted, and they were visiting the campus where they believed he would attend college.

I wish we—or anyone—had detected and thwarted the killers' plans. Yet *nothing* was as simple as many wanted to make it seem in retrospect.

I've seen childhood pictures of the killers. They grinned through lost teeth. They proudly wore their soccer uniforms. Those pictures don't match up with the image I still see in my mind of a teenage Harris pointing a gun at me. These two kids didn't come out of their mothers' wombs hating, so what happened? How did they become killers?

We may never know.

Chapter Nine

Recovery

As the memorial services continued, news reporters scrambled to try to break revelatory material about what had happened. Much of it turned out to be wrong.

Columbine wasn't the first school shooting, but with the internet and the information revolution, this was a new world. I'm not advocating that we turn back the clock on progress, but I will say that I think this new age makes it possible to publish content that is rushed, inaccurate, and insensitive.

Media outlets covered the memorial services, graduation, and every move we made. I later learned that when we returned to classes at Chatfield High for the final weeks of the school year and then at Columbine the following school year, some people in the media offered kids money to take video cameras into the schools. They also offered money for 1999 yearbooks and Columbine memorabilia.

The local media, for the most part, acted responsibly. They knew they were a part of our community. Many of the local print and broadcast journalists were deeply impacted by the tragedy, and in some cases, local reporters were courteous enough to let me know about stories that were about to be aired or published so I could forewarn the parents and others involved. Those same local journalists later helped us as we traveled the road to recovery. In addition to reporting on day-to-day events in the aftermath of the tragedy, they started reporting on what was being done to help the members of the school community. Human interest stories were reported. One media outlet did a story about the recovery of Patrick Ireland, "The Boy in the Window." Many local media outlets realized what was reported originally was not accurate. They began correcting the facts. Unfortunately, national media were not as interested in correcting the misinformation they had reported, which is why today there are people who still believe the initial reports.

What I saw then, and later, was that some members of the national media would come in, do their story, and leave us in the wake of the damage they'd done with false, inaccurate, or misleading reports. We had to deal with the aftermath. Note I said "some." Many national media members helped us during the road to recovery.

Kiki Leyba

66 *There was never a moment when I doubted that Frank was not just my principal but also my leader. He was my mentor. He led us. He was a voice of calm. The fact that he was so visible was reassurance. As things began to unfold, the finger pointing started almost immediately, and he was a shield for not just our staff, but also our community. He was very willing to stand up in front of a microphone or a camera and take on all of the stuff that was coming at us. You didn't see a bunch of our staff doing interviews. We allowed—we wanted—Frank to be our spokesperson.*

"We all recognized, as the days turned into weeks and months, that he was burning it at both ends. PTSD sets in pretty fast, and I could see it happening to him. I knew he wasn't sleeping, and being awake gave him more time to think about it. You could tell. His body language . . . well, he'd be a terrible poker player

"He could tell us things; he never gave us false information, but you could tell he was laying everything on the line, that he felt a responsibility in all of this. You could see it on his face, you could see it in his posture. But he just kept going, and he never wavered. He never ducked the community. He was true and loyal to his community, the families, the neighborhood, the feeder schools, everybody. He was a leader. I'd follow the guy into a burning building. I mean, I watched him run toward gunfire. I'll never forget that. I have that image burned into my brain. From that day forth, he never wavered."

About a month after the killings, an FBI agent finally took me back to the Columbine library, still considered a crime scene. Momentarily, I was numb. I felt nothing. I blacked out. It was denial. But when I checked back in out of that fugue state, the agent showed and explained to me how each of the kids killed there had died that day.

That still sticks with me.

Shortly after that, I decided I wanted to get some things out of my office and straighten it up, and I asked LuAnn to join me for support.

LuAnn DeAngelis Dwyer

" I had bought him a geranium when he first became principal, and it stunk like coffee because that's where he'd empty

his coffee. That was there. All of a sudden, he said, 'Come on, let's take a walk.' He'd start and stop, and he'd say, 'That's where they came in.' We'd walk a little ways, and he'd say, 'This is where Dave Sanders and I were,' and he'd stop talking. He'd stare. We held hands and walked down into the room where Dave had been. And then into the library, and he knew where everybody had been, where Patrick Ireland had gone out, where the librarians had been in the cabinets. He'd talk about the flooding from the sprinklers and the papers floating. He talked about all that, but he didn't mention those other two. Again, what we learned was that if he talked, we listened. We never brought anything else up. 🙶

As we went through the final days of the school year at Chatfield, I was getting the feeling that kids felt they couldn't (or didn't want to) share their feelings and experiences about all of this with their parents. Concerned about their sons and daughters, parents called me. One parent stated, "Even though my son survived, I have lost my son. He has changed." Parents begged me to talk to their children because they knew that I had a good rapport with them and perhaps could encourage and help them to open up to their families. So at an assembly one afternoon I gave them some advice. I said, "This is not going to make sense to you until you're parents, and that better not happen any time soon. But when your parents heard there was a report of gunfire at Columbine, their hearts started racing and their stomachs sank. They weren't sure they ever were going to see you again. Your fathers were wondering if they would ever walk you down the aisle on your wedding day. Your mothers wondered if they ever would have a chance to hold their grandchild. You need to go home, and you need to love your parents and tell them how much you appreciate them. This doesn't make sense to you right now, but it will."

That talk came full circle for me in August of 2011 when former student Michelle Romero Wheeler visited my office. She was weeping uncontrollably. When I asked what was wrong, she said, "Mr. De, remember when you met with us and talked about someday being parents?" I said, "Yeah." She said, "Today, my daughter started kindergarten. I walked her to school, and I grabbed her hand and started squeezing. She said, 'Mommy, you're hurting me.' I let go. All of a sudden, when she was about to walk through the door, I ran up to her. Everyone was looking at me, and I grabbed my little girl, and I clutched her to my chest. My daughter said, 'Mommy, you're scaring me. What's wrong?' All I could think of was when she went into that building, was there any possibility that she may not come back out?" Other students who were survivors who are parents now are experiencing similar emotions and are trying to decide what they will share with their children about that horrific day. The fears that cut into our lives on April 20, 1999, never fully leave. Healing and time lessen their effects, but those scars are always there . . . and sometimes, as they did for Michelle that day, the fears resurface, and the wounds reopen.

Exactly one month after the killings, President Bill Clinton and First Lady Hillary Clinton attended another ceremony at Dakota Ridge High School. As President Clinton addressed the students and families, faculty, and the first responders who came to the school, he said, "When America looks at Jefferson County, many of us see a community not very different from our own. We know if this can happen here, it can happen anywhere. And we see with admiration the fundamentally strong values and character of the people here, from the students to the school officials to the community leaders to parents."

That day, he told me privately, "Frank, we will help you build whatever you need." He backed that up, even after his presidency. He made several more trips to help us raise funds for the Healing of People Everywhere (HOPE) Columbine Memorial Library and the Columbine Permanent Memorial. He called me several times to check to see how I was doing and sent letters of encouragement and a copy of his 2000 State of the Union address. He greatly helped me and our community with the healing process.

The 1999 commencement was two days later at Fiddler's Green. There were probably 14,000 people in attendance. Murder victim Lauren Townsend was one of the valedictorians. Her mother, Dawn Anna, and her stepfather, Bruce Beck, came up, and I presented them with a diploma along with a cap and gown. Lauren and Isaiah Shoels were the two victims who would have graduated that year.

I worried about the Class of 1999. That class had no idea what was confronting them. It all had been so sudden. They went off to college, and many of them struggled to find the support they needed. Life was difficult for everyone who had been at Columbine the day of the shooting. And for the kids and staff members who returned for one, two, or three more years, it was tough. But we had each other.

At times, I still felt sorry for myself and would ask, "Why me?" I put an end to my pity parties by spending Saturdays at the world-renowned Craig Rehabilitation Hospital in nearby Englewood, Colorado. I spent my time there with four of the Columbine wounded. Their lives had changed forever, and seeing them fight to recover put my own life in perspective. Patrick Ireland had to learn how to walk and talk again. Anne Marie Hochhalter was paralyzed as the result of being shot in the back as she sat in the stairwell. Richard Castaldo was right next to Rachel Scott, and his wounds left him paralyzed from the waist down. Sean Graves was only fourteen. A bullet had pierced his body, and he had no movement or feeling in his legs. He was discouraged, and his mom and dad were understandably worried. When I visited Sean, I said things like, "Don't give up hope, you have so many kids who care and love you. We're looking forward to the days when you return to Columbine High School. You are serving as inspiration." It took a long time, but by his sophomore year, Sean was able to return to Columbine in a wheelchair.

In addition to seeing the strength of those I visited on Saturdays at Craig Rehabilitation Hospital, my faith, church, family, and friends helped me get through the rough months and years following the shootings. Forming trusting relationships and maintaining faith have been at the heart of my life, and that was crucial, not just in the immediate aftermath but as years passed. My counselor, Patrick Maloney, not only provided mental support, but as a member of my parish, he also provided spiritual encouragement.

Even as things began to normalize for me, there were times when I realized my life would never be the same. One of those times was July 4, 1999, when the fireworks went off at a Rockies baseball game. I reacted reflexively, getting in the fetal position and crying. Nobody outside my family noticed that, in an instant, I was back in the hallway with bullets flying all around me.

We returned to the Columbine building in August for the 1999–2000 school year. Prior to the shootings, I had hired thirteen teachers for the next year. Before classes started, I called each one of them and told them if they didn't want to take the job, I understood.

They all came. Only a few staff members retired or left after the 1999 school year. District leadership allowed every staff member the option to be transferred. I was grateful that a majority returned; we needed each other.

For a long time, we weren't sure if the building was going to be ready in time for us to return. I got back into my office in July while the school was still considered a crime scene. The district had agreed to major renovations. Contractors were in the building virtually around the clock. More than once, while working in my office, sounds from the ongoing construction triggered emotional reactions in me.

During the first couple of weeks back in the school that summer, I'd walk down the hall as I had with LuAnn. Every step took me back to what I had experienced that day, and I'd have to turn back. Each day I was able to get a little farther down the hallway. Maloney encouraged me to think of the victims as vibrant kids. So then, and later, as I walked the halls and saw the names in my office, I imagined Lauren Townsend playing volleyball. I saw Rachel Scott on stage. I saw Danny Rohrbough as a freshman, just being a freshman, hanging out with his friends. I saw Isaiah Shoels high-fiving me. I saw Danny Mauser and Kelly Fleming down at church on Sundays. I saw them all. I envisioned them living their lives. That's the thing that kept me going.

I never thought of leaving Columbine. I knew I had to be there. As Father Ken had said, I had a mission, a charge, a task ahead.

LuAnn DeAngelis Dwyer

❝ Here was this one guy who was going to stand up there by himself to rebuild it if that's what it took. But he didn't have to. ❞

Anthony DeAngelis

❝ I truly believe it was the Columbine community that helped him through it. The teachers and the parents were there to help him rebuild. That was the strength. They saw how he took hits from the press and how he didn't let it be about *that. He said, 'That's not what it's about now,' and he waited. We were going to support him in any decision he made, but I think he felt that if he quit, he quit on them. He wasn't going to do that.* 🙶

Rick DeBell

🙶 *I never said, 'Frank, you have to get out of there.' I never pushed, never tried to second guess him. I know how he grieved, and I know how we felt about that community and about Columbine. I would always say, 'It's your call, Frank; if you want to stay, stay. You know what's best—for the community, for Columbine, and for the future students.'* 🙶

I've thought about why I stayed. I also know that with the ways the social climate has changed in this country, things might be different for me if the shooting had happened in the last few years of my principalship. Now, with the political arena and knee-jerk reaction on social media being what they are, I doubt if I would have lasted in the job. Back then, although the media coverage was intense, things were different. Plus district leaders Jane Hammond and Jon DeStefano supported me, along with students and the community. Later, Hammond's successor as superintendent, Cindy Stevenson, backed me too. Jon and Cindy were two of my strongest supporters throughout my career. (As are so many I worked with during the Columbine recovery, Jon and Cindy are dear friends of mine to this day.) I learned valued lessons on leadership from Cindy. Chief Academy Officer Sherida Peterson also offered friendship and support. In effect, the district leadership said I could stay as long as I wanted—as long as the healing moved forward.

Yes, there were some people who wanted me out of there. Some local media members were after me. It was interesting that, once I got to know some of those critics, we developed relationships, and their opinions of me changed. The primary example was talk-show host Peter Boyles. Initially, he ripped me, but after Jefferson County Schools Executive Director of Communication Rick Kaufman contacted him and suggested we go to lunch and talk, we became friends. In fact, Boyles became one of my strongest supporters and dearest friends. Now I know if I need anything, Peter is just a phone call away.

Fortunately I had developed positive relationships with many of the members of the media prior to the tragedy, and they knew the type of person I was; many knew me as a teacher and coach. Dave Logan is one example. Dave's accomplishments include but are not limited to (1) being one of two men drafted in all three major-league sports, (2) having a productive NFL career as a wide receiver with the Cleveland Browns and, briefly, the Broncos, (3) winning state championships as a high school football coach with several schools in the Denver area, (4) holding down a radio job as a talk-show host, and (5) serving as the Broncos' radio play-by-play voice. (Yes, mostly all at once!) As a Wheat Ridge High pitcher in 1972, he plunked me with a 95-mph fastball in a non-league game when I was playing for Ranum. He doesn't remember it, and I don't hold it against him. Dave's support, on the air and in private, meant a lot to me. In addition, Lee Larson, the president of media giant Clear Channel Communications, founded the Never Forgotten Fund, which annually provided thirteen scholarships for twelve students and one teacher in the state of Colorado. Support from people like Dave and Lee along with so many others from the community further affirmed my decision to stay on as principal of Columbine High.

Chapter Ten

Changes

We all acknowledged the need to avoid constant reminders of where much of the violence and murders had occurred. The library was closed, and we used a temporary library building, placed outside the main school, for nearly two years.

We began fundraising to build the HOPE Columbine Memorial Library as a replacement. In May of 2000, workers tore out the floor of the old library and put in the atrium. The new library opened in April 2001. But even as those modifications were only in the planning stages, we returned to the school.

I helped lead a "Take Back the School" rally that also included parents, community members, and alumni in the senior parking lot. I made sure to portray the rally as a tribute and triumph of spirit. "I have waited for months to say this," I said to the crowd. "Columbine, we are back!" I added, "My door is always open to you. You are all my children, and I love you."

I had to wipe tears from my eyes.

Then I said, "At Columbine High School, we will have zero tolerance for cruelty, harassment, excessive teasing, discrimination, violence, and intimidation." To me, and I believe to the students, that statement simply emphasized our existing and long-standing policies. It was important to get that on the record, but some took it as admission that the killers had been maltreated. That inference was wrong.

After the rally, Patrick Ireland and teachers who were on staff when the school opened in 1973 led students and staff members back into the school, and our flag was raised to full staff for the first time since April 20.

By all accounts, the rally had been a success, but when it was over, I knew had I made one of the worst mistakes of my life that day. It's one I still regret and will take to the grave with me. Wanting to emphasize the upbeat, I decided not to read the names of the thirteen dead at that rally.

The advice I had gotten was mixed, and I listened to those who said we needed to move forward. As the principal and leader of the school, I was open to considering advice. At times the advice was valuable; other times I had to listen to my heart. I wish I had listened to my heart on August 17, 1999. I later took some criticism for not reading the names and, as well-intentioned as I was, I deserved it.

As soon as I got in my office, I started crying because I knew what I had just done wasn't right. I contacted as many families who lost their loved ones as I could, apologizing and promising that their children and Dave Sanders never would be left out again.

"What I did was wrong," I said. "I wish I could do it all over again, but I can't. All I can do is ask you to forgive me. Those kids never will be forgotten. I won't let it happen."

From then on, I made certain that honoring the murdered was a priority and that it would go hand-in-hand with emphasizing community and recovery. I recite their names every morning. When I speak publicly, I show their pictures and recite their names.

Principal school doesn't prepare you for recovering from a school-wide crisis of the magnitude we'd suffered. Things would be going along as normal, and then something innocuous would trigger those horrific memories. We quickly realized, for example, that we couldn't serve Chinese food in the cafeteria because that was the menu on the day of the murders; the smell was another reminder. When we had fire drills, maybe four hundred or so wouldn't participate, because they were too traumatized. We had to ban camouflage clothes because many of the first responders were wearing camouflage clothing when they entered the building. Teachers had to change their lessons, and there had to be precautions taken to avoid re-traumatizing students. War videos could not be shown, because the sounds of gunfire would be wrenching for students. Some of the novels previously used in courses had to be abandoned because the stories felt too closely related Columbine's trauma.

Some of the kids were uncomfortable with the strictness of our policies. One had a T-shirt made that said, "If we offend, they suspend." We knew why we had to do it, but sometimes common sense was thrown out. It was all black and white, and some kids came up and said they were uncomfortable, mentioning that Columbine wasn't a school, but a fortress. To a point, they were right; indeed, the enforced policy was zero tolerance. Looking back, my administrative team and I probably went too far, disciplining students for minor incidents. But we felt it was what we had to do.

Some students, though officially enrolled, were homeschooled. A lot of parents didn't want their kids at Columbine that year and, to a lesser extent, the next few years. But I truly believed Columbine was the safest school in the world after the tragedy because we had so much security. We had additional police officers and parent volunteers at every door. And because of federal grants, we had additional security cameras throughout the building.

The teachers were the true heroes. They returned to classes while they were still struggling themselves. They took care of our kids. The staff members of 1999 will always have a special bond, and even though we struggled as individuals, we forged ahead as a group. We knew: We are Columbine! We are Rebels for Life! Those teachers will always hold a special place in my heart, and I am eternally grateful they were with me during the good times and the bad. The tears we wept and the laughs we shared allowed us to heal together.

As we got back into the groove of school, I repeatedly emphasized the need to be open to getting help. I'd say to teachers or kids, "I don't know about you, but gosh, I'm having a hard time sleeping, I have no appetite, and I'm having these bad dreams." Whether it was during a student rally or at a staff meeting, I'd always see people nodding in agreement. Despite the initial (bad) advice I'd gotten, I talked openly about seeing a counselor. I think that was better than hitting people over the head with the idea of getting help. I think, especially for guys, there's this misguided macho idea that we need to handle hard times on our own. That's just not true. There is no shame in talking to a counselor, therapist, coach, or psychologist. Many staff members thanked me for modeling behavior that helped them heal. My actions were granting them permission to get help, to cry, to feel the way they were feeling. The more staff members talked, the more they realized others were experiencing similar emotions and reactions. Tim Capra had been teaching special education at Columbine since 1995 and was also the boys' and girls' golf coach. He was one of those who let me know later that when I said it was okay to get help, he also sought counseling.

I had a few people tell me, "I talked to someone, and it didn't help." My answer to them was, "You need to find the right person." I have also had people tell me, "I don't need anyone. I have friends, and I talk to them." They often said they also had their spouse or significant other and their parents. But my response to that was, "If you break your arm, are you going to that friend, spouse, significant other or parent and have them put pins in it or a cast on it?" There are times you need to talk to someone with the professional training to help you work through your thoughts and emotional wounds. When I travel, I tend to reflect when flight attendants say something along the lines of, "If the plane loses cabin pressure, an oxygen mask will drop down. Put the mask on yourself before you help someone else." This is the message I share: You cannot help someone else until you help yourself.

The healing process was long and littered with well-meaning catch phrases. People came up to the kids and said, "I know how you feel." The kids were resentful. They'd think, "How the hell do you know how I feel? You weren't hiding under a table." Or teachers would think, "How the hell do you know how I feel? You've never stood between a killer and twenty kids. You were never held hostage for hours, with lights flashing and the fire alarm blaring, wondering if you will ever see your loved ones again. Do not tell me how I feel."

I understand that people who offered words like "I know how you feel," were only trying to be helpful or empathetic. But here's a suggestion: There are a lot of times when bad things happen, and you just don't know what to say. In those moments, I've learned that not saying anything and instead just being there for the person who's hurting is the best thing. When I met with the parents of the Beloved Thirteen, or the parents of the injured, or the injured kids, I never could say, "I know what you're feeling." I didn't lose a child or have a child injured in the shooting or feel a bullet rip through my body. No, I didn't know how they felt. But I knew they were hurting; we all were. And I knew that being there for the students and staff helped me as much as it did them.

We were on the way back. But there would be setbacks too.

Chapter Eleven

Our Hearts Will Go On

The NBA Denver Nuggets, NHL Colorado Avalanche, and baseball's Colorado Rockies cancelled games in the wake of the Columbine tragedy.

The Avalanche even agreed to open a playoff series against San Jose on the road, rather than at home, a major competitive concession.

The Rockies provided a field for the Columbine baseball team to practice. Sean McGraw was a 1988 Columbine graduate I had taught when he was a student and coached when he played on our first baseball state championship team. He worked for the Rockies, and he invited me to a Sunday game against the Arizona Diamondbacks. When I arrived at the stadium, he introduced me to Rockies manager Jim Leyland, who presented me with a plaque that listed the names of the Beloved Thirteen. He said the Rockies organization offered its condolences and that the Columbine community always would be in the organization members' thoughts and prayers. The president of the Rockies, Lakewood High and Colorado State graduate Keli McGregor, continued to support

Columbine High and be a friend to me until he passed away on April 20, 2010.

Another Rebel, Bryant Winslow, who was also on the state championship team in 1987 and later on the College World Series championship baseball team at Wichita State, stepped up to the plate. His family construction company, Winslow Construction, helped build the Dave Sanders Memorial Softball Field.

The Columbine Alumni Association, headed by Curt Bigelow, was instrumental in helping us through the road to recovery.

Denver's Pepsi Center, the home of the Nuggets and the Avalanche, was set to open in October 1999. The opening act featured singer Celine Dion, whose husband, René Angélil, was the best friend of Avalanche general manager Pierre Lacroix. Lacroix lived near Columbine and, along with several Avalanche players, was very supportive in the wake of the shootings. On that opening night at Denver's new arena, Celine invited Columbine's vocal music group to her concert to sing with her. Our choir director, Leland Andres, asked me to join them as a chaperone. I jumped all over that!

We arrived early enough on the evening of the concert for the students and me to watch Celine's pre-show rehearsal. Afterward we went to a team locker room where we met a few Avalanche players, including Claude Lemieux and Joe Sakic, who were on their way to the concert. Celine walked into the room next, and I have to say she is the nicest person you'd ever want to meet. I made a star-struck fool of myself. When I held the camera upside down while taking a picture of Celine and some of the kids, we all had to laugh when she teased me, saying, "This guy runs your school?"

When it was time for the concert, those of us who weren't on stage had some of the best seats in the house. Our vocal group joined us when their part with her was over. As Celine and the Columbine Students sang, "Our Hearts Will Go On," there wasn't a dry eye in the house. It was a special evening for everyone in attendance but had such special meaning for our Columbine family. As the concert was ending, one of Celine's representatives came over and told me she had invited us to come to her reception. We got more pictures during the reception, including one that hung on my office wall for years. And it turned out that she donated all the proceeds from the concert to the Columbine mental health foundation for Columbine victims. Celine and the Avalanche's generosity helped us as we continued on the road to recovery. Other performers reached out to us too. Shania Twain invited our Jazz Band to join her on stage at Fiddler's Green to perform. It was a special day for us when Big Head Todd and the Monsters, which included 1983 Columbine graduate Rob Squires and 1984 graduates Todd Park Mohr and Brian Nevin, performed a song for us at Red Rocks Amphitheater at a community event the day before we resumed classes at Chatfield High School.

Another unforgettable moment from that first school year back came when Columbine won the state football championship. The team that had been wrongfully and indirectly accused of being a factor in the killers' motivations helped bring the school together with a storybook-style victory.

The Rebels trailed Boulder's Fairview High 17–0 in the fourth quarter of the quarterfinals . . . and won 21–17.

The Rebels trailed Cherry Creek 14–0 early in the championship game . . . and won 21–14.

After the final game, I was interviewed during the celebration on the field and told the reporter, "This team never quit. It's not about not giving up, and that's what Columbine High School represents."

It was a moment of joy in the middle of a hard year. But even during the fanfare and celebration, those we'd lost were on my heart. So it really shook me when one reporter I spoke with said,

"This [winning] really changes things." I thought, *This is just football. We lost thirteen lives.*

Our coach, Andy Lowry, was standing next to me, saw the look on my face and jumped in and told me he didn't think the reporter intended to come off as insensitive and as cavalier as that sounded. All the members of our Columbine family struggled with feeling guilty if we celebrated any event. The families of the murdered were so inspirational and supportive in helping us heal. Ann and Joe Kechter, parents of the murdered Matt Kechter, and Matt's brother, Adam, were at the state championship game and were in the locker room for the celebration. There were tears of joy and tears of sadness. Despite everything, we were being careful not to make a football championship more than it was—and yes, that involved knowing that there still were some buying into the myth that athletics ran Columbine. We knew what was being tossed around out there about the Columbine culture.

Were there some jerk athletes over the years? Yes, there were, but they don't represent every kid who played an athletic sport, just like there were some kids in the performing arts who weren't model citizens. But that didn't mean every kid in the performing arts or the marching band was bad.

Humans have the tendency to paint with broad strokes and miss the full picture. What I saw was a team that dedicated the season to Matt Kechter, a terrific kid and brilliant student who was a sophomore at the time of the shootings. He was among those killed in the library. Had he lived, he would have gotten significant playing time during the championship game. His younger brother, Adam, a middle school student, was on the sideline during the awards ceremony. When he held up the trophy in honor of his brother's memory, well, between the celebration and the commemoration, the emotions were overwhelming. It took me back to a moment from Matt's memorial service earlier that year when, in a statement read to the mourners, his parents, Joe and Ann, told us, "The greatest gift of remembrance you can give Matt is finding the courage and the strength to rebuild your school and your community."

We were trying.

Every time we seemed to take a couple of steps forward as a community in the recovery, though, we took a step back. In October 1999, Carla Hochhalter, the mother of paralyzed Anne Marie Hochhalter, walked into a pawnshop, asked to look at a pistol, loaded it with bullets she had brought with her, and shot herself to death. A detective came to the school and told me. In disbelief, we pulled Nathan, Anne Marie's brother, out of class so the detective could take him home and break the terrible news about their mother.

On February 14, 2000, two Columbine students, Nick Kunselman and Stephanie Hart, were murdered at the Subway sandwich shop where they worked. Their murder remains unsolved. And although it may have had no connection to the shootings in 1999, the senseless loss of young life rocked our world again.

We were shaken once again in May 2000 when Greg Barnes, a standout basketball player and exceptional student who had been with Dave Sanders when he died, hanged himself. Greg was one of the students who had tried to help save Dave's life by trying to stop the blood loss. He had even pulled out Dave's wallet and showed him pictures of his family while they waited for paramedics to arrive. Greg's service was held at St. Frances Cabrini, the same church where funerals had been held for Kelly Fleming, Daniel Mauser, and Matt Kechter. Over the years, when I attended others' funerals at St. Frances Cabrini or other churches, I couldn't help but think about all my kids whom I buried; the memories were difficult for me and others in the Columbine community.

Beyond the thirteen who lost their lives that day, there were so many others who were deeply impacted. Our lives were changed forever. Later I realized that the loss we all experienced wasn't unlike the pain of losing a family member—multiplied many times over. When someone you love dies, people bring meals; they're there for you. But when the company goes home, the hurt is still there. Year by year, the pain, at least on the surface, seems to lessen, but it remains. Of course, trauma affects people in different ways. Some of the wounded have gone on to surprise people with their grit and determination to not let that awful day define them. But even now, almost two decades later, some Columbine graduates still struggle with post-traumatic stress disorder. I've seen and talked with students and staff members who were coping and seemed to be doing well, but then an event in their lives triggered emotions that they hadn't experienced the previous five or ten years. Some of the "kids" (they are in their thirties now) still come to see me to talk and remember even as they try to move on. I continue to try to help former students who are struggling; the funds provided for counseling ran out long ago.

During that first year, I sensed that many people believed they would wake up one morning and everything would have returned to normal. I knew that wasn't possible. I told the faculty that Columbine never could be a "normal" high school again, and that was something we had to accept (perhaps while redefining *normal* for our circumstances). That message is one I've since shared with other grieving communities, including Santana High School, Red Lake, Virginia Tech, Chardon High School, Sandy Hook Elementary, Arapahoe High School, La Loche High School, Reynolds High School, Sparks Middle School, San Bernardino, Freeman High School, and Marshall County High School.

Earlier I mentioned how I felt about the class of '99 and how its members had to go off into the world without the same built-in supports as the other students. They graduated on May 22, a little over a month after the shooting, and they had to deal with the unknown as they either started jobs or went off to college, trade school, or the military. The daily interactions with the Columbine family were gone, and the support in their various ventures was not there. Life was difficult for the Classes of 2000, 2001, and 2002, but we had each other. We had a support system in place. Most people don't understand how it feels when triggers bring traumatic memories and emotions to the surface. For these students, that lack of understanding or support for what they were going through, both in the immediate aftermath and in the years to follow, had a negative impact on many of their lives. Some denied that the problems they experienced were related to the shootings. They had a difficult time with the college course workload. Many were away from their families and looked for support to get through the tough times. They sometimes turned to alcohol or drugs for that support.

Through experience, I have learned that the hurt never fully disappears. In fact, those feelings of fear and hurt may increase if they are avoided or ignored. In 2012, it became even more apparent to me and others that members of the class of '99 were still struggling. On July 20 of that year, a gunman opened fire in a movie theater in Aurora, Colorado. Immediately a group of Columbine survivors mobilized to support the survivors of that shooting. This group of former students still carried feelings of hurt, anger, and fear. They understood the feelings that those in the Aurora community were experiencing, and they tearfully shared their own experiences as they empathized with them. After witnessing how the graduates, specifically the class of '99, responded in the wake of the Aurora shooting, the need for long-term support after such crises became clear. The result of this realization is The Rebels Project (named in honor of the Columbine mascot). The group reaches out to other survivors in ways that only others who have been through similar experiences can. The mission of The Rebels Project is to embrace, support, and connect survivors of mass tragedy and trauma by creating a safe environment to share unique resources and experiences and provide education surrounding the varying effects of such trauma. I am proud of the Columbine '99 graduates who founded the project: Zach Cartaya, Heather (Egeland) Martin, Jennifer Hammer, and Stephen Houck. I'm proud of the important work they are doing.

Among the many who offered their support to the Columbine community was Gerda Weissman Klein, a Holocaust death camp survivor liberated at age seventeen. Soon after she was freed, she married an American soldier, Kurt Klein, who had been among her liberators, and came to the United States. Both Gerda and Kurt were invited to Columbine after Gordon and Ellin Hayes, social studies teachers, spoke with Sandy Friedin (McDougall Littell Publishing's sales rep to Columbine) and company president, Rita Schaefer. Her visit on January 20, 2000, was life changing for our school community. Soon after her visit, she sent us a letter. In it she wrote,

> Being with you has brought back many memories of moments in my own life when I was your students' age and was confronted by the same senseless hatred and loss that resulted in so much pain. But along with the unspeakable cruelty, I also witnessed many acts of incredible humanity, love and sacrifice . . . . You, the young people at Columbine, will, I am sure, be able to turn the barbarism you have seen into acts of kindness and caring. Thus, Columbine will forever be a symbol of humanity and redemption.

Gerda made several more trips to Columbine and provided a great support for our community. Her words rang true, but our emotional wounds still festered. I knew our students and staff were struggling during those first few years after the shootings; I was right there struggling alongside them. I often forgot to eat (or just didn't feel like eating), and my weight dropped to 134 pounds. Several times in the three years after the tragedy, I headed to the emergency room thinking I was having a heart attack, only to find out it was anxiety that had made me feel as if I were dying. After one episode, I apologized to the doctor profusely. But he said, "Frank, the first time you think it's anxiety, it could be a heart attack."

It seemed as if everybody needed me. I was fine with that; it was what I wanted. But the pressures mounted, and I kept too much of it inside. The effect of that stress showed up for me physically. It also took a mental toll. In about the first ten years after the shootings, I was in roughly six automobile accidents, always in the month of April. Distractions mounted in those months as I reflected. Eventually I visited my counselor, Patrick Maloney, each April for what I called maintenance. I had his number on speed dial.

I tried to be proactive about my own healing. Talking with my counselor helped. I continued to attend Bible study with my spiritual partners at Columbine, perhaps looking more for strength than answers. We all learned there was no timeframe for the healing process. People were in different places mentally and spiritually. Trying to meet the needs of everyone was a monumental task. I was putting up a brave front. I allowed myself to show emotion. I had never had a problem with that. I've often said that because I'm Italian, I get emotional at the opening of a Walmart. But inner turmoil lurked beneath the displayed emotions.

Anthony DeAngelis

" This definitely has taken a toll on Frank. No ifs, ands, or buts. He went through a time, and we went through it with him. It was to the point that when we went out, he would not have a drink. He was so criticized by people, and he thought that with all the cell phones, we could be having a beer, and it would be all over, and people would take it wrong. "

One bright spot during those years was becoming a grandfather to Vinnie, Leah, and Rayden. Being a grandfather was wonderful and they provided fond memories. But day to day, my marriage bore the brunt of the pressures and stress that eventually caused my wife and me to divorce in 2002. Now I understand that while trying to lead the healing and being involved with so many, I too often shut out those closest to me. I should have involved family members, including my wife and children, in my counseling so they could better understand what I was experiencing. I learned that avoidance is not a good coping mechanism. I am going to repeat this: Now, whenever I mentor administrators, I can't stress enough the importance of balancing professional and personal lives.

Chapter Twelve

Hate Is Too Great a Burden to Bear

I received as many as twenty-five letters a day following the shootings—written letters, since this was before e-mail was pervasive. At first, I tried to read them all, but I found I wasn't putting much of a dent in the backlog. At the urging of Patrick Maloney, I eventually decided to put the boxes of mail aside because among the cards and notes from well-wishers, there also were just enough hurtful and hate-filled messages to distract me from my mission to lead our school community to healing.

As that mail and other communications reflected, while the school community generally rallied in the wake of the tragedies and supported me in my efforts, that unity wasn't complete. I had my own unreasonable and virulent critics, who posted caustic and hateful comments on the online newspaper articles about me. These critics took their shots at me daily using the (then) new internet forums that allowed unfiltered, unmonitored, and frequently anonymous comments.

I'm proud to say I continued to be respected in the community and school, but some members of the public chirped away without being subjected to standards of accountability, accuracy, and fairness. They ignorantly maintained I should have been able to step in and prevent the Columbine tragedy from happening. I was criticized as a "jock principal," and not just by those who bought into the bullying myth. Some folks, even within the community and the school, kept bringing up my background as a coach. When they'd say, "You make sure you go to all the football games." To which, I'd agree: "Okay, I'm at the football games, but so are you. Why aren't you at the school play, school musical, band, and vocal music concerts? You're blaming me for stressing the importance of athletics, but when was the last time you were at a forensic debate or event? I'm there."

Being involved and attending all sorts of school functions was a pattern for me as principal even before April 20, 1999. I found that when I challenged folks that way, a few of them started showing up at non-sports school events. The media showed up at a few too. In the years following the shootings, I knew it was more important than ever for me to be at those events, not in response to the haters, but to be there for the kids. I wanted them to know I was always there for them.

I didn't let the hate mail drain my resolve or ruin my love of education and kids. I refused to allow negativity into my life. Honestly, I was afraid that if I did, I might never recover. My kids needed me. I remembered historian Alice Earle's wisdom: "Every day may not be good, but there's something good in every day."

I often looked at one condolence card sent to me by one of my mentors, Joe Domko, with a handwritten quote from Pope John XXIII: "One may hate the sin, but not the sinner." I had a tough time with that, but I didn't hate. I can never forgive the act. We buried thirteen people. I get angry every time I see the people whose lives were forever changed that day, people who have to live without their child, loved one, or friend. But I also realized early on if I allowed hatred to be pent up in my heart, it stole my energy and capacity to serve the two thousand kids at Columbine and all the kids who were going to follow them. I could not allow the Beloved Thirteen to die in vain. I couldn't allow that anger to fill my heart, because I wouldn't be able to fulfill the promise I had made to rebuild the community.

Not everyone took that approach. Grieving families of some of the killed and wounded were justifiably angry, even embittered. They wanted to feel as if they'd gotten back at least a tiny bit of what they had lost. I completely understood. The families were seeking answers. They wanted to know the truth. Fifteen lawsuits were filed against the Jefferson County Sheriff's Department as the first anniversary of the shootings approached, just beating the statute of limitations for that type of suit. I realize in most cases they were in search of information leading up to and surrounding April 20, and also hoping that the more we knew about what happened, the more it might help prevent future massacres.

More lawsuits followed. Eventually, I was named in eight. Although I believed that naming me in those lawsuits was mostly a catch-all approach mandated by lawyers, it was difficult to take. People said, "Don't take it personally." But when you're named in lawsuits and served with papers, you tend to take it personally. The families who lost children didn't file lawsuits against me; they came from parents whose children had been injured that day.

Now, please understand, I would never, *ever* criticize anyone about the decision to file a lawsuit like that. I've never lost a child or had a child injured the way they did. But I do know I would have done anything to save those kids that day. I believe those kids—my kids—always knew I loved them. When some questioned or said I had no idea who my kids were and that I didn't care about them, that hurt. They were wrong—100 percent wrong. I had my faults as a leader, but I can unequivocally state that I loved my kids and would do anything for them. One of my strengths as a leader was the relationship I had with my kids. So, yes, I was defensive when some seemed to question my loyalty and love for them.

Eventually, families of the murdered and wounded settled suits against the killers' parents and the two young men instrumental in the sale of a submachine handgun to the killers. Also, the Jefferson Sheriff's Office settled a lawsuit filed on behalf of Dave Sanders' daughter for $1.5 million. Most other suits were dismissed. I never was found liable.

Again, I understood that families of the murdered were searching for answers and demanding accountability, especially calling into question the procedure that forced officers to remain helpless outside rather than allowing them to go into the building where they could have potentially saved lives. I didn't feel it was right, though, to criticize the Sheriff's department for following the accepted national protocol in perceived hostage situations. One tiny positive in all of this was that the protocol was examined and changed. I stressed the need for such change when I was asked to testify in front of Governor Owens' Columbine Review Commission. I know that some officers were ready to challenge their commander that day and break protocol to go into the building. In the wake of the Columbine tragedy, the protocol eventually became for the first officer or officers on the scene to engage the perpetrator as soon as possible or prudent.

In May 2001, I found myself back in the spotlight when the Jefferson County Sheriff's report on the events of April 20 was issued. It happened again when the governor's commission released its report. The sheriff's report, understandably, was defensive and needed to be evaluated skeptically, but I'll admit it was a useful and detailed examination of the day's events. Overall, the governor's commission was well meaning and thorough, offering worthwhile common-sense recommendations. But it also was too willing to perpetuate the "bullying" myth. That angered me. Once again, I make this comment because I was privy to The Basement Tapes and journal entries in which bullying was not mentioned.

While the arguing and accusations flew around me, I tried to lead the recovery.

Chapter Thirteen

Reeling, Recovering

In late 1999, *Time* ran a cover story on the two killers. The article included pictures of the weapons they used to terrorize the school. It came out during the first semester of the first school year following the shootings, and our community was traumatized all over again. I don't say this as a criticism of *Time*, a reputable and responsible publication. It's simply a statement of fact. That national publication of our nightmares is just one of many incidents that made it clear we weren't going to be left alone to recover in peace.

By then we had learned that once a story was posted online, it could be refuted, ridiculed, or debunked, but even deleting it or correcting it didn't undo the damage. Years later, the initial mistakes and myths in some cases still live on and are more stubbornly prevalent than the subsequent corrections. I often was angered and dismayed to notice that a few cavalier writers misquoted me, fitting my comments to their agenda—and those false quotes live on in web searches.

Someone told me to never get in an argument with anyone who buys ink by the barrel, but I sometimes had to. I soon realized that even if I did not speak to a reporter, he or she was still going to print the story; therefore, it was important for me to give my side for the story. It was frustrating at times when I would do a three-hour interview and then read the story to see that only a few sentences were used, and they were twisted to put a slant or angle to the story. Things were so many times taken out of context.

On the first anniversary of the shootings, *Today* and CBS's *Early Show* broadcast live from Columbine. We decided to hold a school-wide memorial at 11:20 a.m., and we invited the Class of 1999 to join us. We held a private assembly in the gymnasium and then walked over to Clement Park for the memorial ceremony where the names of the thirteen dead were read. That day I told the crowd, "Whether as family or friends, teachers or fellow students, we all share in this great loss. We miss them now, and we always will."

President Clinton called me to offer his condolences.

During the Class of 2000's commencement the following month, I listened as Patrick Ireland, who still had bullet fragments in his brain, delivered one of the valedictorian speeches on behalf of the four hundred and thirty-five graduating seniors. He had made remarkable progress since his stay at Craig Hospital. It was an especially emotional moment for both of us when I handed Patrick his diploma.

I called for a moment of silence to honor the three from that class who never got to cross the stage: Rachel Scott, Corey DePooter, and Cassie Bernall. I did the same thing the next two years as well, honoring the murdered members of the classes. I also held private meetings in my office with those parents if they wanted to receive caps and gowns and diplomas. The meetings were emotional and I wanted them to realize I never would forget their children.

As I was getting ready for the 2001–2002 school year, I again had a chance to move to central administration or go to another high school, not necessarily as principal. Some officials wondered if after helping Columbine through the immediate aftermath, and given my health issues, it might be good for me to leave. They meant well. I was living in Highlands Ranch; I took some time to think about the suggestion that one day while walking my golden retriever Maggie. I came home and told my wife at the time, "I'm going to stay until every kid that was in elementary school and in middle school that day graduates." I was relieved. I was sticking to my promise. The relief came from having made the decision after having been in a state of uncertainty about the future.

Healing was a journey. Individually and collectively, we took a few steps forward and then stumbled backward. Sometimes we fell, but we always got back up. Terrible memories and moments of joy intertwined daily. Case in point, at a time when my personal life was in shambles and my marriage was dissolving, I was invited to participate in the torch relay that was part of transporting the Olympic flame from Atlanta to Salt Lake City for the Winter Games.

Steve Davis had been the public information officer for Jefferson County during the Columbine tragedy, and we had grown to be friends. He left that position and went to work for the International Olympic Committee (IOC). One day, he called me and said the IOC thought it would be a great idea for the torch relay to come by Columbine. Davis told me the committee members had watched the recovery and believed Columbine would be a symbol of the human spirit.

I checked with the Jeffco School District security folks, and we all agreed it was a great idea. I also learned I had been nominated to carry the torch for one segment of the relay. The protocol was that you carry the torch for a leg where you lived, so for me, it should have been Highlands Ranch. Steve told me that Patrick Ireland and John Tomlin, the father of murder victim John Tomlin, also had been nominated, and officials agreed to bend the rules for us. (None of us lived near the school.)

Since we were already breaking protocol, we bent the rules just a bit further. Patrick was handed the torch at Raccoon Creek Golf Course by Clement Park, and he walked with it down Pierce Street. The crowd went crazy. Once he passed it on to me, he stayed with me on Pierce Street. After two-tenths of a mile, past the school, I passed it to John Tomlin, and the three of us stayed together for John's leg the rest of the way down Pierce Street.

It was Columbine solidarity.

As the three of us walked, students along the route chanted, "We are . . . Columbine!"

Some of them held a banner that said: "Run, Run as fast as you can. You can't catch Mr. De. He's the Olympic torch man!"

When reporters asked for my thoughts on the experience, I told them, "It's a great day for the community and quite an honor. It means a lot to the Columbine community. It's symbolic because the Columbine community has had a torch to bear for the last thirty-three months."

Buoyed by the Olympic flame experience, I decided I was ready to start reading the boxes of mail I had set aside since 1999. One of the first envelopes I spotted and opened was from Diane Wethington, the high school sweetheart who had broken my heart. She had married, had children, and divorced. At the time, my own divorce was in motion and would become final soon. My first thought was, *My God, what did she think of me for not replying?* She had sent me the card back in April 1999. I still remembered her parents' phone number, so I called and asked them to put me in touch with Diane.

Diane DeAngelis

66 I'd been divorced thirteen years when the Columbine tragedy happened. I sent him a card that had my maiden name on it. I told him my thoughts and prayers were with him and that if he needed anything to let my family and me know. So fast-forward three years; he's going through a divorce, and he comes upon my card. He called my mom. My mom, nicely, would not give him my number. She said, 'Let me get your number.' Now at that point, I hadn't really dated anybody for about ten years, because my kids were really involved at school at Northglenn High, and I didn't date, so I could attend all their events. I always said that once the kids got to be eighteen, I would go out on the web or whatever. But when that time came, I decided I wasn't going to do that. I said a guy would have to fall from a tree into the front yard and mow the lawn; that's how much effort I was going to put into dating. I had a really good job; I was fine without a man. But when Mom gave me his number, I thought, 'Well, I'll just give him a call.' We just picked up and started talking. We decided that since he was going through a divorce, and he was a public figure to some degree, we would just talk on the phone for a while. My father was a semi-invalid at the time, and all of my siblings were taking turns giving my mother a break at night. So I would talk to Frank for hours on end at night. My friends said, 'You should just meet him to see if there's a spark or anything.' I went, and there was still the spark there, and we decided we would go back to talking on the phone until the divorce was final in May. My father passed away in April, so Frank came to the visitation and rosary. And the rest was history. 99

LuAnn DeAngelis Dwyer

" *It was a huge relief. There was a smile on his face, and there was hope and love again for him. I slept better knowing there was somebody there for him.* "

Anthony DeAngelis

" *I joke with him that at least we didn't have to hear about him becoming a priest again. We didn't have to go through that cycle . . . Diane didn't even know about that. We told her that she couldn't leave him, because he really would become a priest. We know that.* "

It was fantastic to be reunited with the Wethington family—Diane's mom, Rosemary; and her younger siblings, Kevin, Dan, Eric, Mark, and Maureen. We were all much younger in the seventies. Diane's family has provided so much support since she and I reconnected. I greatly enjoy the time Diane and I get to spend with the Wethington family. My in-laws and my nieces and nephews have truly enhanced my life. I can't help but think back to my high school days when Diane and I were dating and of the interactions I'd had with her siblings. I cherished those times on 74th Avenue, and I'm glad that forty-five years later, we are still making memories. I also look forward to the Dempsey family reunions on her mother's side of the family.

Our second-chance love story in middle age evolved into a relationship that has endured. Moving ahead in the story, I'll tell you that after a long second courtship, we were married in 2013. Diane's support has been indispensable and inspiring as I've coped with personal and professional challenges. She has been my rock. A friend told me she keeps me real, and I love her unconditionally. I would not have been able to fulfill my promise to stay at Columbine for so long without the support of my beautiful wife and soulmate. The Lord works in mysterious ways, and I am so thankful He put Diane back in my life.

Diane DeAngelis

66 *It was Christmas 2013. Frank was always so romantic, even if he had been possessive when he was seventeen. We were at my mom's house, where I had lived when we were dating in high school. Once all the festivities were over with the Wethington family, Frank and I got in the car to leave. He headed in a different direction from where I lived. I asked him where we were going, and he told me to wait and see. We ended up in the spot where we had 'parked' as high school sweethearts. He got out of the car and went to the trunk and came back and presented me with a dozen red roses. He then proceeded to pop in a Jackson 5 CD with our song from high school, 'Oh How Happy.' He then reached into the back seat and brought out a bag with a teddy bear inside. The engagement ring was attached to the teddy bear. He asked me to marry him. I said yes! He never gave up!* 99

At the 2002 commencement, the seniors were from that last class comprised of students who had been at Columbine in April 1999. The four-colored tassels honored the four murdered members of the class: Steven Curnow and Daniel Rohrbough from the shootings at the school; and Stephanie Hart and Nick Kunselman from the Subway sandwich shop killings. Before calling for a moment of silence, I reminded them of the words that had brought me comfort for the past few years: "When a loved one becomes a memory, the memory becomes a treasure. We will treasure the memories of our loved ones for a lifetime."

During my address, I told the class, "You were forced to grow up far too quickly, and you were denied a normal high school life. I wish I could take away the hurt that you experienced during your years at Columbine High School. I wish I could wipe away the tears you had to shed, and I wish I could lighten your heavy hearts and heal the wounds that were inflicted on you."

I thanked them for supporting me and the recovery effort.

"I am eternally grateful, and I love you," I said.

Sean Graves got out of his wheelchair and, using one crutch, walked across the stage to receive his diploma. The crowd erupted with applause. "Here I am, Mr. De," he said. "I'm here to get my diploma. Thanks for never giving up on me." Instantly, my mind when back to the days I spent visiting him at Craig Hospital where he had wondered if he ever would walk again.

Tearing up, I gave him his diploma.

That's what Columbine represents: tenacity and resolve.

Kiki Leyba

66 *He would always do trivia questions at the end of our faculty meetings. If you won, you got something like a gift certificate to the school store. I submitted a question for him one time, and he thought I had given him some bad information and that the question and answer had been wrong. Sometime later I was sitting at my table at a parent-teacher conference, and one of the security guys, Tony Antonio, came up and said, 'Hey, Kiki, can you come with me?' So I followed Tony, thinking this wasn't typical. We went upstairs towards the gym and then into the hallway toward the weight room. Now, I know Tony, and I'm asking what's going on, and he just says, 'Come on.' So I go in there, and the weight room is completely dark.*

Black. At the back of this weight room, back in the corner, there's a light shining down. And there is Frank. He's sitting in a chair. He has a couple of his administrators—big guys—with him. They're standing behind Frank, and they have their arms crossed. Tony reaches into his pocket, pulls out this little tape recorder, presses a button, and the theme from The Godfather *starts playing. I'm like, 'What the hell?' Frank says, 'So you crossed the Godfather. You gave the Godfather some bad information; now you have to pay for it.' I said, 'I wouldn't do that, Godfather.' I couldn't believe that was the length he would go to get a little payback. And I swear to this day, I didn't give him bad info.* 🙶

As the years passed, and I remained principal, I emphasized the positive. More than ever, I participated in school assemblies and events and would poke fun at myself when I served as a guest lecturer in classes (beyond my annual Jonathan Edwards sermon). We were on the road to recovery.

Chapter Fourteen

She's Oprah

I was heartened that the community not only accepted me staying at Columbine, it generally embraced me. I still was "Mr. De" to these kids. There wasn't one morning when I didn't awaken and think about what had happened. I needed to be part of, and to lead, the healing.

The anniversary pattern became familiar. Each April 20, if it fell on a weekday, Columbine was closed, with no classes, but staff members would be at the school. We would provide breakfast and have a staff meeting, but it was a day that meetings were not planned, and they would take care of their needs. Throughout the years, former students and staff members stopped by the school. I would also extend an invitation to the parents of the Beloved Thirteen and the students who were injured and their parents. At 11:20 I would read the names of the thirteen and hold "a moment of silence."

Anniversary coverage was extensive the first three years. Soon, although I still was on the job, the students who had been in the Columbine hallways that day moved on. Many came back to visit me and were in the audience in Clement Park, adjacent to the school, when President Clinton spoke at the 2006 groundbreaking at the park for a Columbine Memorial honoring the murder victims, and again when the memorial was dedicated a year later. I had the opportunity to share the stage with President Clinton and Dawn Anna, Lauren Townsend's mother, who was spokesperson for the victims' families. She was a source of strength for me and for all involved. Dawn is a true inspiration for the members of the Columbine community and for the world.

President Clinton had fulfilled his promise to help with the rebuilding, including when he helped raise money and made a private donation to the memorial. It didn't open for eight years after the shootings, because we wanted to take the time to do it right. We wanted input from the families. We knew we didn't want the memorial on school grounds. Fortunately the park adjacent to Columbine had the perfect spot for the memorial. If you climbed up Rebel Hill, you could look down onto the memorial, where each victim was honored; you could see the school. Of course, we had a memorial plaque in the new library, but the huge memorial on school grounds would have been too jarring. The beautiful memorial in the park, conducive for prayer and reflection, was perfect. Foothills Park and Recreation, under the leadership of Bob Easton, was part of the Columbine family and made the memorial happen.

In April 2008, I had to be hospitalized with a pancreas issue, and it tore me up to have to miss an assembly. I hated not being able to be at school on April 20 that year, but was thankful to have Darrell and Sandy Scott, Rachel's dad and stepmother, visit me in the hospital. It meant a lot to me. That day from the hospital, I called the members of the families who had lost their thirteen loved ones. I will continue to call them for the rest of my life. They never will be forgotten.

Tom Tonelli

" Right after De missed that week of school, we ended up driving to a district meeting together, and I said, 'De, let me ask you a question: Before you got sick, how many days had you missed since everything happened?' He stoically—almost embarrassingly—said, 'Not one.' I said, 'De, there's something wrong with that.' He said, 'Well, I've been out of the building because . . .' I cut him off and said, 'I'm not asking you if you've been out of the building because of a district responsibility. I'm asking you how many days have you missed?' He said, 'None.' Now, he was an overachiever and worked too much and took too much on himself before everything happened, but there was no way he was going to let anything happen when he was not on watch after April 20th. That is when I realized how much of a burden he was carrying. He was taking on a responsibility that no one could carry. I mean, the guy couldn't even leave the school because he felt that if something happened, he would be responsible. "

The district made budget cuts. Columbine actually received $225,000 less funding in 2007–08 than in 2001–02. We wanted to make sure our students received the opportunity for a quality education, as did students in surrounding school districts. So we had funding challenges to overcome, and it led to the founding of the Frank DeAngelis Columbine High School Academic Foundation in 2008. Its initial organizer was the energetic Mary Tedford, whose two children soon would graduate from Columbine, Ben in 2008 and Maddie in 2011. Her husband, Todd, was an original board member and a great supporter.

Other Jeffco schools had undergone upgrades in waves, thanks to approval from the voters, but when it came to be our turn, the results at the ballot box were surprising.

Mary Tedford

The 2008 bond issue didn't pass. Columbine, Green Mountain, and Pomona were all supposed to get multi-million-dollar upgrades in technology and everything else. So we said, 'How can we make this work?' We were frustrated and brainstorming, and we knew that an academic foundation was probably the best way to go. All of the sports at the school had their own booster clubs and raised money that way. Parents get behind athletics, but that support can get lost in academics. You have a hard time getting everyone behind it when it comes to donating money to make your school academic. Both my kids were very active athletically, so I'm not knocking sports at all. Ben played football and played at Colorado State, and Maddie was a lacrosse and basketball player. We believe in athletics and in the importance of them, but we saw that the push was missing for academics and raising money to improve the school, especially in the technology area. So there were a handful of teachers (Frank, obviously) and parents, and we went through the process of becoming a 501(c)(3), and we launched it in the fall of 2009. Our goal is to raise $25,000—which is not a lot—every year to keep upgrading and help the school have money to spend on things it wouldn't normally have money for.

I considered the name of the foundation to be a huge honor.

"We knew that eventually Frank was going to retire," Mary explained to the members of the community. "At that point, we didn't know when, but calling it that just made sense." (Yes, that foundation still exists, and fundraising continues. The website is chsaf.org, and donations can be made there.)

The tenth anniversary came in 2009, and the coverage was extensive both in advance and also that day of the ceremony at Clement Park; in fact, the rush to put together the best anniversary coverage would have been considered farcical had it not been such a serious subject.

Stories of Columbine's remembrance, recovery, and resilience would have been just as pertinent on any anniversary, but the hook of the tenth was irresistible for media outlets. We knew we'd need to have some sort of commemoration. We wanted the families of the murdered to have input and be involved, and we started setting up meetings well in advance.

The event was bittersweet. We had invited everyone who had been at Columbine in 1999 as well as alumni from the 2003–2005 classes to a breakfast. For the Class of '99, that was their first time back into the building since retrieving their personal belongings after the tragedy. On my way down to say hello and address the crowd, I looked out the window down to the cafeteria, and saw *my kids*. Yes, after all this time, they're still my kids. But they were also adults. They had their husbands and wives with them. They had their little kids. They were laughing and joking with one another.

In the time it took me to finish walking down the stairs, I changed my entire speech. I thought there would be more tears and raw emotion, but finally, something had changed. While we would never forget those who were murdered, that day I saw that we had gotten through it. We had indeed survived. Ten years later, we were there to honor both the memories of the victims and what we, the survivors, had become. It truly was a time to remember and a time to hope!

Oprah Winfrey was supportive back in 1999; following the tragedy she had Isaiah Shoels' dad, Michael, and Rachel Scott's brother Craig on her show. It was very emotional. She remained supportive throughout our healing process.

As part of the tenth anniversary furor, I was a guest on the *Oprah* show. It was taped in advance so it could air on April 20. They wanted me to appear with the two lead investigators, Kate Battan and Dwayne Fusilier, plus Dave Cullen, who wrote the book, *Columbine*. I was told they were going to talk about the Beloved Thirteen. I told them I couldn't be out of town that week, or even the week before, because it was prom week, and I was seldom out of the building in April, so they set me up with the Chicago studio in a satellite feed from my office.

As the taping began, I was dismayed to realize that the approach of the show seemed a repeat of the too-familiar sensational focus on the killers and their motives. It wasn't a story on the Thirteen.

When they went to commercial breaks, they would read a name and say something brief about the victim, but that was it.

In the Columbine community, and I would like to think beyond, our belief was that it was more important to remember those who had lost their lives and the twenty-six who were injured. I wanted to tell the stories of recovery, courage, and resilience of those who had been wounded physically and emotionally.

When we finished the taping, an assistant producer came on the feed before I disconnected. Unhappy with the direction the show had taken, I said, "I have to tell you, this is not what we expected. There is so much going on in this community right now; this is going to re-traumatize. This is a slap in the face to the Beloved Thirteen."

"I'm sorry you feel that way," she replied.

I went on to say that if I had known what it was going to be, I wouldn't have cooperated. As it was, I would need to scramble to alert the families and so many others that this would be more of a look at the killers than the victims.

She replied that they wanted to do this show to help parents understand that they needed to deal with kids having issues and not be oblivious. To which I said, "You can do that story anytime." At the anniversary, re-traumatizing the Columbine community wasn't the way to go. I was experiencing many emotions, anger, disappointment, and sadness. I was concerned about the impact the airing of the show would have on our school community.

Our prom was the next day, and we were at Invesco Field, the Broncos' stadium. The phone reception wasn't great, or I hadn't noticed my phone ring, or both, and I noticed a missed call and a voice mail notification. I checked it.

"Mr. De, this is Oprah."

She asked me to call her back.

(I'm a geek. I recorded the message off the phone, and I still have it.)

With the hubbub going on around me, I asked some security officers if there was a private area where I could make an important phone call. They directed me to one, and I dialed the number.

"Oprah, this is Mr. De," I said. She told me she had called because she had heard I had some concerns about the show.

I laid out my case. The families were facing a lot of anxiety because of the tenth anniversary, and we were under the impression that the show was going to be about remembering the victims. I could tell from the taping, however, that it had gone another direction. I repeated what I had told her assistant producer, about bracing the families and trying to mitigate the emotional damage. In fact, I had already informed the Jefferson County Sheriff, Ted Mink. Ted was a friend and strong advocate for Columbine, who, like me, had graduated from Ranum High School.

"Mr. De, I respect you," Winfrey said. "We're not going to run the show."

I said, "That's why you're Oprah."

I was so grateful. I promised her I would let the community know what she had done, and the local newspaper let people know what had transpired.

Chapter Fifteen

The Eye of the Tiger

As the student body turned over, I worked with an evolving faculty as teachers on the staff in 1999 left and others arrived. By the time I retired, of the one hundred and forty-five teachers and staff members at Columbine on April 20, 1999, I was one of only twenty-three remaining. We had a bond. If an event occurred that might have traumatized them, I could walk by their classes and give a thumbs-up, and they'd nod their head—and they would check on me from time to time too.

I enjoyed talking to the students and staff at assemblies. It started at my first homecoming assembly in October 1996. As my career continued, I delivered more and more "Papa De's Lessons," whether in classroom visits, on the public-address system, at assemblies, or just about anywhere on school grounds. The most notorious ones were my increasingly goofy stunts at pre-homecoming assemblies which were tied to the dance's theme.

The homecoming stunts began in 2004, when I rode into an assembly on a Harley with Bruce Stoeklen, a business teacher at Columbine who had been my classmate and teammate at Ranum.

The kids loved it. Even though they were crazy antics, I somehow would be able to turn the theme into life lessons.

One year, the theme of the dance was "Eye of the Tiger." We showed the scene from *Rocky III*, where Rocky Balboa wrestles a very menacing and seemingly genuinely angry Hulk Hogan.

Then I came out as Rocky.

I ran up the steps of the bleachers as if they were outside the art museum in Philadelphia. Unlike Rocky, I could barely breathe. Then I came down and stepped onto a mat to wrestle the school's heavyweight, senior Travis Duffy.

Before the assembly, Travis asked me, "Shouldn't we script something?"

"Nah, we can just wing it," I said. Bad idea.

I came right after him and grabbed him by the ankles, and he started dragging me. Then he picked me up and spun me overhead. The kids were yelling and screaming and the lights were flashing in my eyes (and head).

When he slowed, I said, "Travis, if you don't let me down, you'll never graduate from this high school."

He threw me down gently, and I eventually pinned him. "Papa De's Lesson" was about challenges, appropriate as I had taken on someone twice my size.

The year that the homecoming theme was "New York City," I came into the assembly as Frank Sinatra in a little motorized taxi. Wearing a fedora, I climbed out and sang, yes, "New York, New York." Badly.

I dressed as Willy Wonka. I had on the goofy hat, and as happened in the movie, I put the cane down and did a somersault. I forgot to take off the hat. I wasn't sure I ever was going to get up.

In the "Copacabana" year, I came in on a flat, wearing a white suit and a blond wig, and "playing" the piano as Barry Manilow. My rendition of "Copacabana" brought down the house.

I didn't say it was any good.

I said it brought down the house.

My "Papa De's Lesson" that day was about the choir teacher at Mount Carmel telling me I was so bad, I needed to lip sync. So I told the kids at Columbine that was why I was so afraid to sing in public. And now I was in front of seventeen hundred kids, singing Barry Manilow. Talk about overcoming fears.

Kiki Leyba

66 *You could hear a pin drop in that place when he spoke at the assemblies. Go find a principal who quiets a gym like that. He just had a way with this community. You can't fake that. You can't order that; it just is.* 99

Tom Tonelli

66 *Let me give you an example of how the students at Columbine felt about De. Never mind the standing ovations at graduations or assemblies. The story that sticks out to me is that six or seven years ago, there were a couple of kids— good kids, just mischievous—who had pushed the envelope. An administrator had told them they needed to do something to make the situation right, or they would be punished. The students came to me and said, 'We're seniors; it's second-semester, and we're not going to do it.' I was between a rock and a hard place. I tried to defend the administrator, but the students were having none of it. Then one of the kids said, "If 'De' asks us to do it, we'll do it.' So I said, 'Why would you do it if De asks you?' And the kid's response spoke volumes. He said, 'Because we all know he loves us.' That stuck with me because I can't imagine that is how most kids in public schools feel about their principal.* 99

Diane DeAngelis

" *He has given his life to Columbine. I went to a lot of things with him. But we lived on the North Side, and he would get up at 4:30 in the morning and work out five days a week and go down to school. I'd never seen anyone work like he did. He's not a quitter. I think he did the right thing by staying. I think that community needed him to stay. And I think it was healing for him to stay. He needed that time for him to heal, and he needed that time to prove to himself that he was still the same person. He's risen above the criticism, the crap. Nobody else could have, I don't think. And he doesn't hold grudges. He prays about it.* "

When Columbine was in the state football playoffs again in 2011, the game-week pep rally included an emotional singing of our new alma mater. It closed with:

We are Columbine.
We all are Columbine.
Let the world be told,
Blue and silver we uphold,
Forever.

The Rebels beat Jeffco rival Lakewood 41–31 at (the renamed) Sports Authority Field to claim another state title. Our starting guard, Nick Burns, was a second-generation Rebel. His father, Michael, had played for our 1981 state runner-up team. Nick was five at the time of the shootings and was a member of the Class of 2012, the one involved with my promise to stick around long enough to hand diplomas to all in the Columbine feeder system in 1999.

Nick was profound on the field after the game.

"My dad has strived to instill some of the Columbine traditions and values in me since I was a little guy," Nick said. "I just can't be more excited to bring one home for him and for our family. The tragedy is something that has caused our community to grow so close together. It makes these moments special, more so than I can possibly express. Nothing good will ever come from that day, but this community has come back. Things like this can show the world that, you know what? Even though the worst things can happen, we're going to move forward. We're going to bounce back; we're going to come together. We love each other. Because we are Columbine."

The night before the game, Nick was named the winner of the Matt Kechter Memorial Award, which went to a Columbine offensive lineman of high scholastic achievement.

By then, Matt and the other twelve Beloved each had a place of honor at the Columbine Memorial. Nick knew all about Matt Kechter.

"He's a guy we absolutely all try to emulate," Nick said. "It's important to remember what he stood for. This is why we're out here."

That's why I still was there.

I had promised the football players they could toss me in the air at the celebratory assembly, as college students often do with fellow students at games. They did it, and I said it was about trust—I trusted they wouldn't drop me. The football team tossed me in the air, caught me, and tossed me up again. The players were my trampoline.

Every day, in every assembly, classroom, and hallway, my message was clear: I loved the school, and I loved my students. My "Papa De's Lesson" mixed the serious and the not-so-serious.

Through the years, I became a better principal, and I say that knowing that if you're not getting better every day in a job, you should look for something else to do. I know we all are tempted to find people to tell us what we want to hear. I tried to go beyond that. Some people assumed my efforts were a response to the killings, but they weren't. I often was asked what I was like as a principal before the shootings, and I said I was the same person I was after. I might have had faults as a leader, but my love for my kids never wavered.

Sure, I met with and talked with the student leaders and others who proudly shouted, "We are . . . Columbine!" at rallies and assemblies. Truly, we are Rebels for life. But I was also intentional about seeking out the kids who hung out at the "smoking pit" at Clement Park as well as those at the nearby skate park and the mall food court. These were the kids who weren't necessarily buying what I was selling, and on their own turf, they weren't reluctant to tell me that. They felt disenfranchised, and I genuinely wanted to know what it would take for them to feel a part of the Columbine spirit.

The first time I walked over to the smoking pit at the park, the kids scrambled to put out their cigarettes until I said, "You're not busted!"

They challenged me, asking if I even knew their names. (In most cases, I did, but there were a few I had to learn.) They also asked if I even cared about them. I said, of course, I did. It broke my heart to know there were Columbine kids who still didn't feel a part of the Columbine family. One of their complaints was that they felt as if every school assembly seemed geared toward the 4.0 students who participated in clubs, activities, and athletics. Rather than hash things out in the park, I told them we would pick a date, they could tell all their friends, and we would meet in the auditorium for an hour and talk about how they felt about our school— and what we could do to make sure everyone felt included and loved. They talked, and I listened. When the meeting was over, I think (*hope*) they knew they were my kids, too, and that I cared about them. I invited them to the next assembly.

That meeting—probably one the most important meetings I held in my career—was eye-opening for me. Those kids told me things I did not want to hear, but needed to. I appreciated their honesty and courage to speak up. I asked them to come to the next assembly. One leadership lesson I've learned is that leaders exist throughout the school. They might not often be the traditional leaders, but they are leaders nonetheless. If you do not recognize their influence and try to turn negative leadership into positive leadership, they can affect the organization in ways you don't want. This is true with the student body and with staff members.

At the next assembly, I had thousands of blue carabiners made with the words "We Are Columbine" printed on them. Each student, staff member, and parent at the next the assembly took one. I then explained that each individual in the room represented a link and that each one of them possessed unique qualities. When you put all the links together they formed a single, strong chain; you had *Columbine*. Then, while the song "We Are Family" played over the speakers, I challenged them to put the links together. One by one, the links clicked together until we turned them into one long chain. There were over seventeen hundred in attendance that memorable day. Like that chain, I explained, we were all connected. I told them that during the good times and bad times, they never were in the journey alone. And the kids got what that meant. So did those in coming years. Each year, I gave the graduating seniors their links to remind them that they will always be connected to Columbine and Rebels for life. And I gave carabiners to incoming freshmen. The chain still hangs in the Columbine halls as a reminder that *everyone* matters. As I present to various groups, I continue to share the story and encourage others to use the links for their organizations. I am proud to state that there are schools, law enforcement, firefighter, and health organizations that have used this activity. They, too, will have a "link with Columbine High School;" they do give us credit. Following the shooting at Marjory Stoneman Douglas High School in Parkland, Florida, I encouraged Principal, Ty Thompson, to give each 2018 graduate a link to remind them that they will always be connected to the high school. I truly believe that we can make the world a more connected place—a world that is tolerant of others. The most important point is to encourage others to make their organizations or group more inclusive.

I had to change the perception of the school—within the school and around the world because it was inaccurate. My goal moving forward was to create a welcoming, non-threatening, inclusive environment. As I shared my feelings each year with the graduating seniors, I told them I hoped they were proud to be graduating from Columbine High School. I said if they were not and didn't feel a part of the Columbine family, I apologized for letting them down. I do feel that a majority believed what we declared: "Once a Rebel, Always a Rebel. Rebels for Life!" The support and love given to us by the alumni in the aftermath of the shootings helped us heal. We are Columbine. We kept saying that loud, and we said it proud!

So, yes, Columbine changed over the years, and I also took pride in this: In a "choice enrollment" district, where students could attend any high school that had spaces available, Columbine's enrollment remained at around seventeen hundred, among the highest in Jeffco. Neither the kids nor their parents shied away from Columbine. I believe I had something to do with that.

We became a success story.

Rick DeBell

❝I think Frank came to grips and to peace with himself. I really do. I felt that he was not going to let Klebold and Harris beat him, and he will not let them do it to this day. ❞

As I handed the students of the Class of 2012 their diplomas, I knew I had fulfilled my promise of staying around until all of the students who were in the Columbine system in 1999 had graduated. But I didn't stop there; I had a parent tell me I could not leave, and I informed him that I had fulfilled my promise. He said, "Frank you do not understand my son was in the first year of a two-year preschool program?" I chuckled and stayed two more years. It did make me feel good to know that the parents wanted me there.

Kiki Leyba

❝ My daughter, Lauren, was in kindergarten in April 1999. She graduated from Columbine in 2012. I have a picture of Frank hugging her at graduation. That picture is priceless to me. ❞

As my career wound down, I received pictures in the mail and in emails from some of the girls I had encountered in the Columbine hallway that day and led back to the gym. They were sharing their lives and their families' lives with me. They realized things could have turned out much differently for them—or could have ended for them that day. They were celebrating their lives—rightly so—and sharing it with me. The pictures were of their kids accompanied by notes of thanks. Recently a few of the parents thanked me for saving their daughters and allowing them the opportunity to be grandparents. One exceptionally emotional encounter occurred when a father of one of the girls shared with me that he was a war veteran and that, in his eyes, I was a hero for saving his daughter. As we hugged, we both had tears in our eyes. I could not help thinking back to that horrific day when the girls and I escaped into the gym. We will share a bond for the rest of our lives.

LuAnn DeAngelis Dwyer

> **❝** *I still tease him, 'You'd probably still be there if there wasn't the possibility of someone coming up and stating, "My grandma said she had you when she was a student."'* **❞**

I was sixty years old when I retired, and I believe my rapport with the kids was still strong. Sure, I occasionally needed help from kids to work my cell phone or get on social media, but in many ways we were still on the same wavelength. They knew I cared about them, and they cared about me. That's the reason I kept coming back.

Chapter Sixteen

A Club Nobody Wanted to Join

O ther school shootings brought the media back to Columbine, and reporters sought comments from me.

Sadly, the list of shootings between 1999 and my retirement is very long.

1999   Conyers, Georgia; Deming, New Mexico; and Fort Gibson, Oklahoma

2000   Flint, Michigan; Lake Worth, Florida; New Orleans, Louisiana; and San Diego, California

2001   Santee, California; Williamsport, Pennsylvania; El Cajon, California; Parkland Washington; and Gary, Indiana

2002   New York City, New York; Milwaukee, Wisconsin; and Jersey City, New Jersey

2003   New Orleans, Louisiana; Red Lion, Pennsylvania; and Cold Spring, Minnesota

2004   Washington, D.C.; East Greenbush, New York; and Randallstown, Maryland

2005   Chicago, Illinois; Red Lake, Minnesota; and Jacksboro, Tennessee

2006   Roseburg, Oregon; Reno, Nevada; Hillsborough, North Carolina; Bailey, Colorado; Cazenovia, Wisconsin; and Nickel Mines, Pennsylvania

2007   Tacoma, Washington; Compton, California; Virginia Tech—Blacksburg, Virginia; Dover Delaware; Willoughby, Ohio; Conway, Arkansas; and Fort Lauderdale, Florida

2008   Memphis, Tennessee; Baton Rouge, Louisiana; Oxnard, California; DeKalb, Illinois; and Knoxville, Tennessee

2009   Chicago, Illinois, Larose, Louisiana; and San Francisco, California

2010   Madison, Alabama; Bladenboro, North Carolina; Detroit, Michigan; Austin, Texas; Salinas, California; Carlsbad, California; and Marinette, Wisconsin

2011   Omaha, Nebraska; Martinsville, Indiana; Houston, Texas; Pearl City, Hawaii; Albany, Georgia; and Fayetteville, North Carolina

2012   Houston, Texas; Chardon, Ohio; Jacksonville, Florida; Oakland, California; Perry Hall, Maryland; Newtown, Connecticut; and Taft, California

2013   Atlanta, Georgia; Santa Monica, California; Sparks, Nevada; Lithonia, Georgia; and Centennial, Colorado

(This is not a comprehensive list as it omits incidents where no one was physically injured, parking lot and drive-by shootings, as well as some incidents that happened after hours, in college dorms, or when school wasn't in session. The list of these horrific tragedies continues to grow even today. In February 2018, seventeen people were killed and seventeen injured by a shooter at Marjory Stoneman Douglas High School in Parkland, Florida. In Texas in May 2018, ten people were killed and ten injured by a shooter at Santa Fe High School. Indeed, it seems that barely a month during the school year passes without some sort of school shooting incident. Sometimes, fear is the only damage. Too many times, however, these acts of violence leave communities reeling in pain and loss.)

In Bailey in 2006, in the foothills of the Rockies to the west of Denver, a deranged school intruder killed Emily Keyes when using her as a human shield at Platte Canyon High School.

As she was being held hostage, her last text to her parents was "I love u guys."

At Columbine, we felt that community's pain. Several teachers told me, "Frank, we need to go up and help them because we had so many people help us."

I went to Bailey and met with the principal, Brian Krause, and the staff. My staff members joined me on several other trips to Platte Canyon High School. A few days after the shooting, I attended a Platte Canyon football game. While at the football game, I met John-Michael Keyes and Ellen Stoddard-Keyes, Emily's parents, and that feeling of heartbreak took me back to April 20, 1999. I became friends with John-Michael and Ellen and helped support the I Love U Guys Foundation, honoring Emily. I now serve on the board. The Keyes family has done remarkable work in providing school safety through the Standard Response Protocol—which calls for lockout, lockdown, evacuate, and shelter—and the Standard Reunification Method. The emergency plan was implemented in Jeffco Schools and is being used in schools around the nation. I'll go into more detail later.

Talk-show host Peter Boyles, my critic-turned-supporter, was instrumental in the success of the Emily's Parade, a motorcycle ride from Columbine to Platte Canyon that served as a fundraiser for the I Love U Guys Foundation. The first motorcycle rally occurred less than two weeks after Emily's murder and was a stirring, emotional experience for all involved. For ten years, the annual and successful fundraiser helped promote school safety. Peter is a remarkable—and very outspoken—man and a great humanitarian who also supports the MCI 1 Run in memory of Jeffco Sheriff David Baldwin, who lost his life on Highway 93 while working, and funds from it support officers injured in the line of duty. Peter also has helped us in supporting a Haitian child, Hope.

The July 2012 theater shootings at nearby Aurora reprised some of the same themes. Twelve died in that attack at the hand of a single deranged gunman. The "No Notoriety" movement has gained strength since the Columbine tragedy. It calls for media outlets to refrain from naming mass murderers, at least lessening the infamy that so many seem to have sought. No Notoriety organizers have their own Twitter account and an aggressive approach. Change was evident during the Aurora theater killer's trial, when the Colorado media reacted and covered it all quite differently than it had Columbine. There was far more attention paid to the stories of the murdered and to the recovery of the wounded. The difference, of course, was that the Columbine killers committed suicide, while the Aurora killer was captured alive and went to trial.

Although the 2015 trial, which ended with the killer sentenced to life in prison with no chance of parole, was extensively covered, the media focused on stories about the survivors and victims, and the public appreciated it. It's an important social shift. Regardless of whether the killers live, commit suicide, or are killed by police, if they get the media attention, others with similar sick mindsets think, "This is the way to leave a legacy." The public can take part in diminishing their fame while honoring the victims and survivors.

Following the shootings at Newtown in December 2012, Kiki Leyba and Paula Reed went out to help the staff members at Sandy Hook. I went in February of 2013 to help, and in May of 2014, Kiki, Heather Martin, Jennifer Hammer, Carolyn Mears, Michelle Ferro, and I returned to continue to provide support. There I passed along what I could about counseling and even coping with renewed attention at anniversaries. It's never easy to visit places where communities have been struck by senseless violence. My own memories of horror come flooding back every time. But sharing what I've learned is one small way to help people through the long grief and recovery process. I am proud of staff members and students who were at Columbine on April 20, 1999, and are willing to help other communities experiencing tragedies.

In the shooting at Arapahoe High in late 2013, a student bent on vengeance went on a rampage against a librarian who doubled as the debate coach. He shot seventeen-year-old Claire Davis, who died eight days later. The day of the shootings, we had to make a decision on whether to go on lockdown since Arapahoe was only eight miles from Columbine. We didn't, but Kiki Leyba, who had attended Arapahoe, and English teachers Eric Friesen, Jason Webb, Paula Reed, and I ended up meeting with teachers from Arapahoe at Columbine to help with their recovery. Kiki and I went to Arapahoe a few weeks later to offer support to principal Natalie Pramenko (who was a friend) and her staff.

Since Columbine, I try to make contact with the schools and communities to offer condolences and to offer help. I remember receiving that call of support from Bill Bond, principal at Heath High School in West Paducah, Kentucky, where a shooting occurred on December 1, 1997. He offered condolences and told me to save his phone number, saying I didn't even know what I needed in the immediate aftermath but that as time went on, I would need advice. He has been a great support for me and we have had opportunities to do some work together. That's the thought I share when I make the first calls.

Each time I receive text messages offering thoughts, prayers, and support, I immediately go to the internet to see where another school shooting has occurred. On January 23, 2018, I made that call to Principal Patricia Greer at Marshall County High School in Benton, Kentucky when two of her students were killed. We have shared several conversations.

After a gunman entered Marjory Stoneman Douglas High School in Parkland, Florida, on February 14, 2018, and killed fourteen students and three staff members, I had numerous conversations with the superintendent's cabinet and with Principal Ty Thompson, sharing my thoughts on what to expect as the healing process began. In addition, I had a phone conversation with social studies teacher Carla Verba, offering suggestions as they planned their graduation.

On, March 20, 2018, a student opened fire at Great Mills High School in St. Mary's County, Maryland, killing a student. I had a phone conversation with Dr. Jake Heibel to offer help following the tragedy and met with him personally in Maryland to help with the healing process and to discuss the upcoming graduation.

On May 18, 2018, a student opened fire at Santa Fe High School in Santa Fe, Texas. Nine students and one teacher died, and ten more were wounded. I had numerous conversations with

Superintendent Leigh Wall, Executive Director Pam Wells, and Principal Rachel Blundell to share my thoughts on what to expect as the healing process began.

Unfortunately, each conversation takes me back to the many days, months, and years following Columbine's tragedy. Each time, my counselor, Patrick Maloney, along with Diane and other family members and friends, provide the support that I need to continue to help others. My faith is crucial too. Each time, I assure those experiencing tragedy that I will be there for them every step of the way.

I only visit sites of tragedies when invited. In the wake of mass trauma and acts of violence, those left behind become members of a club that no one wants to join. It's terrible and excruciating, but despite evil's intent, we end up stronger than we were prior to the tragedy. What people see in Columbine is that we are a school and community that bounced back. If I can walk into schools or walk into communities and create an environment of love, that can help. That's my hope.

Chapter Seventeen

The Last Time

O ur mantra at Columbine about the murdered remained, "Never Forgotten." I kept an eye on the former students of that era and watched them mature while still working with the young people in the Columbine hallways. I helped students experiencing post-traumatic stress syndrome to find funding and support. Once I met my pledge about handing diplomas to those in the Columbine system in 1999, I faced the decision on when to retire.

In 2013, I announced that the next school year would be my last. My first thought had been to try to be like the NFL Colts departing Baltimore for Indianapolis, without fanfare or fuss. Once my last graduation ceremony concluded, I could back up my truck and clean out my office quietly. The next semester, people would ask, "Hey, where's that little Italian guy?"

Superintendent Stevenson didn't like that plan, and I understand why. She wanted my staff, students, parents, and community members to know this was coming. After I left, there would be a new principal—and a transition—for the first time in eighteen years. My successor would be only the sixth principal since Columbine opened its doors back in 1973. The hiring process for a new principal would begin in January. With Stevenson's blessing, I told the staff during the second week of August at the opening day faculty meeting. It wasn't long before word got out to the rest of the community. I did interviews with the local media outlets about my decision. For me, it finally felt like the timing was right. October 1979, when I first reported to work at Columbine, seemed like yesterday. I had been so bright-eyed, naïve, and unsure of what to expect when I walked into Columbine that day and met two of my mentors, Joe Domko and Gordon Hayes, for the first time. My confidants, Chuck Herring and Dale Clark, showed me the ropes that year. They were there every step of the way to make me a better teacher and later a better principal

At fifty-nine I was in relatively decent health, but my hip was bothering me. I went in for a checkup with my long-time Kaiser physician, Dr. John Pearse. Through the years, I had continued to work out and go to my weekly Weight Watchers meetings each Saturday in Arvada. The Weight Watchers routine had become as much about friendship and support as managing poundage. I wasn't in ill health, but Pearse wondered about the rest of me. He said my physical health was good, other than a bad hip, but asked if anything else was going on in my life. I told him I didn't think so, but I knew my days at Columbine were numbered. After thirty-five years there, I would not be entering the doors at a place that I called home. I have been fortunate to have Dr. Pearse as my primary physician for a majority of my career. He has taken great care of me, and I value his advice. Dr. Mark Barcewski, a 1994 Columbine graduate and a member of the last baseball team I coached, is my chiropractor. He keeps me well-adjusted—figuratively and literally. I always am proud to see how well former Rebels are holding together.

Dr. Pearse asked when I had last spoken to my counselor.

Shaken, I called Patrick Maloney.

"Frank, here's the bottom line," Patrick said. "Your head is telling you you're going to retire, but your heart isn't ready. You're afraid, aren't you?"

I was. When you do something for thirty-five years, it becomes part of your identity. That can be true with anything, of course, but I believe it's especially true in education and when working with young people. Patrick told me that Columbine didn't have to define me, but neither did I have to leave it behind in retirement; I could take the story nationally and contribute to an important dialogue about school safety, leadership, and crisis recovery. The more I thought about it, the more I knew it would be a good way to transition to my next phase of life. My decision felt bittersweet. I wasn't just leaving a job I loved; I was leaving my Columbine family. We had been through so much together, and I couldn't imagine my daily life without them. Diane was a huge support in helping me transition into retirement. She has been my rock.

Coincidentally, Jeffco also was losing two other long-time high school principals to retirement, Ralston Valley's Jim Ellis and Lakewood's Ron Castagna. All along, they had been two of my close friends, and I knew they were only a phone call away if I needed anything. I remember calling them on the first day we had students to start the 2013–2014 school year. As our final year approached, we encouraged one another to make it a memorable year. We cherished each day as the countdown continued. The memories of our times together will last for a lifetime. (Ellis and his wife, Dana, now live close to Diane and me, and Ron and his wife, Debbie, joined me as board members for Caruso Family Charities.)

Part of making the most of that year, for me, included allowing Denver's NBC affiliate, KUSA-TV, with anchor Kim Christiansen, education reporter Nelson Garcia, and photojournalist Chris

Hansen, to periodically chronicle my emotional final year on the job. They did a terrific job and created a program titled, *Rebel with a Cause*. The amount of time and, even more importantly, the heart and sensitivity they put into the project were above and beyond the call of duty. They watched. They listened. They filmed. And they got it right. They received three Emmys for their work.

I was selected as the Colorado principal of the year in 2013 and was one of the three finalists for the national high school principal of the year award. I would be joining a hundred of the other state high school and middle school winners for the awards ceremonies. The problem with that was that they were in Washington D.C., and I couldn't be at the Columbine homecoming assembly. It was only the second assembly I had missed in thirty-five years. The other was the 2008 prom assembly when I was in the hospital. Because I didn't want to miss any milestones that year, I got on a Skype call to talk to the kids.

Late in 2013–2014 year, for my final, greatest stunt at a pre-prom assembly, I flew across the gymnasium hanging from wires and pulleys. Diane, my parents, and my stepson, Matt, were there too. I had confessed to the students that I was afraid of heights. Man, was I ever. So this was another way to demonstrate to them that I—and they—could overcome fears and that they had to believe in themselves. I'm not sure my parents ever recovered after attending my final assembly and witnessing me flying across the gym. I owed a special thanks to the school senate sponsor, 1988 Columbine graduate and valued friend Eric Friesen and to Assistant Principal Summer Guerrina for helping make that happen at my final assembly.

My "Papa De's Lesson" at that assembly focused on overcoming fear. "You're going to face many fears in your life. You have to believe . . . . Do not deny your parents the opportunity to see you grow, to have your dad walk you down the aisle, to have your mom hold your first child. I look forward to attending your college graduations and weddings. I look forward to being at your ten-year reunions. Take care of each other and make wise choices because I cannot lose another kid of mine. I love you!"

LuAnn DeAngelis Dwyer

66 *His whole point was, 'If I could overcome my fear, so can everyone else.' It wasn't just talk; it was doing it.* 99

I was emotional because I knew it was the final time my dear friend Ivory Moore and I would be together at an assembly to perform the chant, "We are Columbine!" It took me back to the fall of 1996 when we did it for the first time at my first homecoming assembly. When he finished the chant, we embraced, and I told him I loved him. Reality was setting in, that I had only six weeks remaining before I left my Columbine family.

Something else happened that day that still can make me get misty when I think about it. One of our students, Kevin Yagovane, had been in several foster homes and was estranged from his parents. He was living with his aunt and uncle, and Columbine was his ninth school. Kevin joined us his freshman year. Knowing that it can be tough to start a new school when you don't know anyone, I made a point to personally meet each student who came to Columbine from somewhere other than a Columbine feeder school. Meeting with them was one way I tried to help get them plugged in. Kevin and I checked in with each other every so often. It was great to see how he had found his home at Columbine.

A few days before my final prom assembly, Kevin slipped a letter into my office door's mail slot. I read it at the assembly. He wrote:

Dear Mr. DeAngelis,

Thank you so much for being such a great principal over the years. Though I only had the pleasure of having you as my principal for a school year and a half, you have made a big impression on my life. You took the time out of your schedule to talk to me during my freshman year. We talked about my start at Columbine. Though I was not able to add my link to the chain that year, you truly made me feel a part of the Rebel family with that one talk. My life has been full of nine different principals over the years and has been a fairly tumultuous time. The acceptance and family atmosphere that you helped create here at Columbine has really grounded my life and has helped me create friendships that I will always remember. When I first started school here at Columbine, all my case workers had asked me if I felt worried about being at another new school. I told them that I knew it would be a great school, the greatest I have ever gone to, and that if I had any issues whatsoever, I knew I would have a great person to talk to. You always take your time to say hello to everyone in the halls, and you at least know every student's first name. Thank you for being such a great person and instilling the best school-wide atmosphere I have ever experienced."

With Love and Gratitude,
Kevin Yagovane

When I'd finished reading his letter, I asked Kevin to come down from the bleachers, and I presented him with a blue Columbine link. The students stood and cheered; some even cried. And as he returned to his seat, they offered hugs and high fives.

That was the family atmosphere I had strived to create for eighteen years.

The problem was that everything I did that year—not just that flight in the gym—I was doing for the last time.

My last *this*, my last *that*.

My visitors that spring included NBC's twosome of Lester Holt and filmmaker Sam Granillo, a 2000 Columbine graduate, and they profiled me for *Dateline* and *NBC Nightly News*. In the story, other student survivors talked about how their lives were impacted by the tragedy and what they were doing fifteen years later. Holt interviewed graduates associated with the Rebels Project, including Crystal Woodman Miller, Heather Martin, Stephen Houck, and Zach Cartaya. They continue to reach out to communities after tragedies. Holt had interviewed me fifteen years earlier, when we focused on my friendship with Dave Sanders and the impact he'd had on our school community.

In the final months of the school year, people often asked me if I was counting the days.

I'd answer, "Yeah . . . I only have (x) more days with my kids." I was not excited about retiring, because as each day passed I had one fewer day with my Columbine kids and my Columbine staff.

My friends hosted a tribute roast at Pinehurst Country Club as the school year was winding down. It was both funny and touching. It took a few weeks, but I managed to forgive everyone for their jokes. I had myself to blame. I said I'd rather have a roast than a "tribute" dinner—which would have made me even more uncomfortable—and it was a fundraiser for the Frank DeAngelis Columbine High School Academic Foundation.

"I think Frank had announced to the faculty at 7:30 in the morning that it was going to be his last year," Mary Tedford said later. "And I think at 7:35, Kiki Leyba was on the phone with me, saying, 'We have to do this.' And I said, 'Absolutely.' It was the greatest way to say, 'We Love you, Frank.'"

On the last day of classes, I addressed the kids on the public announcement system:

"Good morning, Rebels. This will be the last time I'll get a chance to address you. Know that even though I'm not going to be your principal, you're still going to be my kids."

I spent a lot of time in the hallways that day signing yearbooks and talking with students. One student I'll call Chris here to avoid embarrassment told me, "Thank you for being more of a father to me than my dad ever was." Everywhere I looked, there were memories to share and students to love. More than twenty former students had joined Columbine as staff members. They, and all my kids past and present, made Papa De proud.

In my office, a sign on the wall had this reminder: *You're a Columbine Rebel for life, and no one can ever take that away from you.* The names of the murdered were on the wall too. Throughout my career, many asked me how I could look at that reminder every day. I explained that I was honoring them when I carried through on the promise to help rebuild that community.

In addition to the picture of me with Celine Dion, I displayed photos of me with President Clinton, Jack Nicklaus, and Rudy Giuliani. There also were many letters of thanks and support from celebrities and non-public figures. A drawing of Dave Sanders, a gift from a student, occupied an honored spot near the door, as did one of Kyle Velasquez's baseball caps, given to me by his parents, Al and Phyllis, who told me, "We cry because we lost him; we smile because we had him." I am eternally grateful for the support of the families who lost their children on April 20, 1999. They will always have a special place in my heart, and those mementoes inspired me to be my best every time I walked out of my office.

Kiki Leyba

❝ I hope that people will have a sense of how he was with us—how he took care of us, our staff. We really felt like that. When he retired, we were sad, but we were also thinking, 'Good. You need to. Go do something fun.' He gave us so much of himself in the years after. His commitment and devotion to that place, the students and staff, the community, was a true devotion. He didn't stay because of guilt; he stayed out of a sense of service and a sense of duty and love, and it was because of who he is and what he wanted to do. ❞

Diane DeAngelis

❝ More than anything, he loved the kids, and I think that's what he misses more than anything. That's why he didn't go to the administrative building. He wanted to stay for the kids. I don't think he should have done anything else. ❞

Finally, and in some ways far too quickly, the class of 2014 crossed the stage. At the last commencement, Area Administrator Dan Cohan read a letter from President Barack Obama:

THE WHITE HOUSE
WASHINGTON D.C.
May 15, 2014

I send greetings to the 2014 graduates of Columbine High School and to your principal, Mr. Frank DeAngelis, as he retires.

For 35 years, Mr. DeAngelis has dedicated himself to the students of Columbine High School. In the aftermath of its darkest hour, he led your community on the long journey toward healing. With remarkable resilience and compassion, he supported families, fostered a nurturing learning environment, served as a beloved principal for 18 years, and stood with communities across our country recovering from violence.

Mr. De, Columbine is stronger and more hopeful today because of your service. Your promise to remain principal until the youngest students at the time of the tragedy graduated high school reflects the best of the human spirit. I am pleased to congratulate you on your retirement, and I hope you take pride in the lasting difference you have made in the lives of so many, and in the special place you hold in the Columbine community.

I am also pleased to congratulate the class of 2014. Your graduation marks the culmination of years of study, and the world needs your unique talents and boundless passion. If you apply yourselves fully to tackling the challenges ahead, I know your generation will prove once more that those who love their country can make it better. As you reflect on all that you have accomplished, I wish each of you all the courage and determination you need to reach your dreams.

(Signed,)
Barack Obama

In addition, I had received letters from Vice President Joe Biden, senators and members of the House of Representatives, plus senators and representatives from the State Legislature. It was overwhelming but greatly appreciated. Also, I received a United States flag with a certificate reading as follows:

This is to certify the accompanying flag was flown over the United States Capitol on April 20, 2014. At the request of the Colorado United States Congressional Delegation, this flag was flown for Mr. Frank DeAngelis in recognition of his 35 years of service, including 18 years as Columbine High School's Principal.

The encased flag and certificate hang proudly in my home office and serve as constant reminders of my time at Columbine High.

A Time to Remember. A Time to Hope!

Chapter Eighteen

Telling the Story

If I had stayed on the job, I would have been addressing the Columbine staff at the start of faculty business for the school year in August 2014. Instead, I spent the end of summer at the Jersey Shore with my mom and dad, my brother and sister and their families, and my wife and our family, and my Jersey cousins, Diane and Bobby McLaughlin and Angel and Tony Librizzi and their families. We watched the tides roll in and walked on the boardwalk. It was much more relaxing than getting ready for another school year. Chuckling, I realized it was like a scene from the show, *Jersey Shore*. My mom was an only child, but I'd had the opportunity to grow up with all my second cousins. I've emphasized this throughout but want to again: My family is of utmost importance to me, and they helped make me what I am today. I love them all dearly.

In the early stages of my retirement, school shootings took place in Marysville, Washington; Roseburg, Oregon; La Loche, Saskatchewan; Antigo, Wisconsin; Townville, South Carolina; San Bernardino, California; and Rockford, Washington. Every time I hear of another horrific incident, I still see our Columbine kids running with their hands on their heads. Every event brings back what we experienced.

Diane DeAngelis

" He does have nightmares. He'll wake up and somebody is chasing him. I'm awakened by the, 'No, no, no,' and I'll have to wake him up. He has nightmares pretty often, actually. I'll say, 'What was that about?' He'll say, 'Somebody was chasing me with a knife.' It doesn't seem to affect him; it's not something he sits and broods about. "

One lesson I have learned is that the unimaginable is possible. And as horrific as it seems, we must prepare for the unimaginable. You have to have a plan. Winging it is not a plan. Attacks are happening at businesses, churches, movie theaters, and shopping malls too. No one is immune. Now, more than ever before, those in education must proactively prepare for the worst.

At least now, we're working as a team. Education leaders, counselors, teachers, and parents are starting to understand that we're not looking for a single red flag, but for pieces of a jigsaw puzzle we can put together. School, family, law enforcement, the judicial system, the business community, and the community in general today pool knowledge and effort.

We have increased security measures at schools: Designated entries, more security officers or staff members dedicated to monitoring entry to the school, IDs, and visitor badges are all part of common place today. Instead of fire drills, schools practice lockdowns. That's a Columbine effect. It's not foolproof. When some of our students argued in the aftermath of the shootings that Columbine had become a fortress rather than a school, they weren't right. But they weren't out of line either. Security measures are tighter virtually everywhere, although in some places there are limitations because of finances.

When I travel to speak and make my presentations, it often is at conferences where organizations demonstrate some of the amazing advances in first-response technology. Much of it is tied to mobile communication and apps that quickly alert law-enforcement personnel—both on and off duty—who have agreed to be part of a virtually instant notification chain. Also, the protocol generally is that the first-responding officers can engage the perpetrator or perpetrators. That's what happened at Arapahoe High, where school resource officer James Englert confronted the shooter within ninety seconds. If not for that, the toll might have been higher. Claire Davis' death was one too many. But Englert's actions—and the change in protocol that allowed him to take the initiative—likely saved lives. Advances in first-response technology are crucial to protecting our schools, churches—any place where people gather. Had some of the modern procedures and applications been in place in 1999, we would not have lost thirteen.

That's one of the reasons I tell the Columbine story. Whether through speaking engagements or larger-scale media context, I want to give people context for what life was like both before and after the shootings. And I want to be sure the story is being told truthfully and respectfully. Looking ahead, as of this writing, 9News Reporters Kim Christiansen and Gary Shapiro are working on a twentieth anniversary package to run in 2019 that will include a television special, daily news stories, and social media interaction with viewers. They asked to meet with the people who were most affected. It was a very emotional experience for the people who met with Kim and Greg and opened up about how difficult the past two decades have have been for them. I know it all will be terrific because of the sensitivity and humility with which they approached the project.

I don't aggressively seek speaking engagements. They frequently come from word-of-mouth recommendation. Depending on the nature of the group, I often donate back any honorarium. The heartfelt reactions and warm receptions from audiences have been encouraging and reassuring. Regardless of the audience, I emphasize the Columbine constituency's strength. I also pass along something Dawn Anna, the mother of murder victim Lauren Townsend, shared with me: "There's nothing we can do to bring back our beloved children or Mr. Sanders, but we are going to do everything in our power to make sure that parents don't have to mourn as Columbine parents did."

If you had told me years ago that something horrific would happen at Columbine, I would have said, "No. No way, not in *this* community." Jefferson County had 162 schools. Of our Columbine kids, 92 percent graduated on time. Our dropout rate was less than 2 percent. More than 88 percent went on to college, with 25 percent of the student body getting some kind of a scholarship. Columbine had advance-placement classes and was an International Baccalaureate school. Those programs meant that some Columbine students walked out the door as sophomores in college in academic standing. It was a community of pride and tradition. There was a lot of parental support. Bottom line: Columbine was (and still is) a highly respected and exceptional public high school. I thought—we all thought—nothing like that could happen to our school community.

After laying all that out to my audiences, the reaction often is, "Frank, your community is just like ours!" The realization that Columbine is so much like their schools and communities helps them understand that no school or community is immune to evil.

When I talk with audience members after my presentations, they share their stories with me. In Oklahoma City, a woman handed me a sticky note with the words, "People may refuse our love or reject our message, but they are defenseless against our prayers." It's true. Prayer, intentional love, and my faith helped me progress toward recovery after the tragedy. I always believed it was important to pray for the people who love you, but I've come to understand that it may be more important to pray for your enemies because of the way those prayers affect you.

Each time I speak, I adapt my message to my audience and even the location, but I always begin by reading the names of the Beloved Thirteen as their faces are shown on the screen. Then I turn to the audience and say: "There's not a day that goes by that I don't think about these thirteen—one of my dear friends, Dave Sanders, and twelve of my students. The thing that makes it so difficult is that they were killed by two of my kids. As I lay in bed on April 20, 1999, I made a promise to those killed. There was nothing I could do to bring them back, but I was going to do everything in my power until the day I die to remember them. They would not die in vain."

One of the most fulfilling speaking experiences came on July 9, 2017, when the I Love U Guys Foundation held the annual Columbine Briefings at Columbine, and I had the honor to open the conference and share the stage with AJ DeAndrea. AJ was one of the SWAT officers involved in the first and second sweeps of the building. It was the first time for us to present together, and it was emotional and healing at the same time. I expect that AJ will join me at additional conferences and presentations. I again was proud of him in August of 2018, when he was promoted to Deputy Chief for the city of Arvada.

Even as my hip deteriorated (eventually, I underwent hip replacement in October 2017) I kept up a busy travel schedule across the United States, Canada, and even to Europe. I have met amazing people, and I still love it when I'm able to present at school assemblies. Kids still are my passion, wherever they are. When I'm speaking to educators, to school resource officers, to firefighters, district attorneys, judges, mental health workers, or others, I enjoy forming relationships with people who share the goal of making schools as safe as possible while facilitating learning in positive, healthy environments.

Initially the air travel and the visits to new cities were very exciting and very new, but now traveling takes its toll. I always feel an exhilarating rush of adrenalin when I get to present at conferences, but travel isn't always glamorous.

A trip to remote La Loche, Saskatchewan, stands out as one of the most eventful. A shooter there killed four: two students in their homes and two teachers at the Community School in 2016. Kevin Cameron, executive director of the Canadian Centre for Threat Assessment and Trauma Response in Alberta, asked if I would speak to the La Loche school community. I agreed, and we set up a Skype call. During that call, one of the school leaders asked if I could visit them in person. I told them I was presenting at a conference in Alberta in November 2016. Alberta was much closer to La Loche than Colorado, but the drive still would have been fifteen hours. That's when they offered me a lift on a four-seater plane.

I had never been on a plane so small, and when the pilot said we needed to move the suitcases and backpacks to balance out the weight of the plane, I was uncomfortable. The weather wasn't great, and we had to wait a while to take off. When we were in the air, the pilot turned around, looked at me, and said, "I can't see where I'm going." He was wiping the inside of the windshield, and he said, "Frank, I know they want to see you in La Loche, but I don't think it's safe."

We turned around.

When I was safely back on solid earth, I called the folks in La Loche. They proposed that I come up in January instead, when we would be able to drive across a frozen lake, making it a reasonable trip. I said yes, and early in our trip, the driver who picked me up in Alberta said, "Gosh, I hope this road is frozen." At that point, I again wasn't feeling real comfortable, but we made it, and it was a memorable ride. I'm guessing the driver was having some fun at my expense. When I got up there, residents were appreciative, and it was a rewarding experience. I shared my story with the members of the school staff. When I told them that I knew what they were feeling, there was instant credibility. They had become members of the club. I stressed the importance of taking care of themselves. As I ended my presentation, I shared my contact information with them, assuring them I was just a phone call away, and I would support them as they continued to heal. On February 21, 2018, I received a text from Principal Greg Hatch, asking me to call him. He told me the killer was scheduled to appear before the judge on Friday, and the members of the community were struggling. He just needed to talk. He later texted me, "Hi Frank. Thank you for your time yesterday! Your support has really helped me and our school. The La Loche school shooter will be tried as an adult." (It is so important that the members of the club reach out during difficult times. On February 27, 2018, I called my friend Andy Fetchik, the principal at Chardon, to tell him I was thinking of him in the sixth anniversary of the shooting. My hope is that he and other members of this terrible club know I am always there for them.)

Another time, I appeared at a conference in Vancouver. The next year, the organizers asked if I could return. I agreed. They gave me the dates, and I booked my air travel back to Vancouver. The organizers said they had made me a reservation at the Marriott and sent me the phone number and confirmation number. As the date approached, I called the hotel number and asked how far the hotel was from the Vancouver airport.

There was a pause . . . then laughter.

The hotel was in Toronto.

I had assumed the conference was back in Vancouver. It was in Toronto. Vancouver and Toronto are 2,725 miles apart.

We managed to get that straightened out in time.

Chapter Nineteen

Something Good from Something Bad

I'm proud that my presentations and consulting have drawn praise because it affirms that I am still helping people. Here are a couple of examples of testimonials about my presentations and consulting:

> Frank takes his experiences from the tragedy at Columbine in 1999 and presents powerful programs on leadership, resiliency, recovery, and a variety of other applicable topics that will grip your audience during a more-than-memorable presentation. His programs (keynote, break-out, or workshop) work for every audience type from healthcare, emergency responders, schools, and general industry.
>
> I had the privilege of working once again with Frank this past week in Orlando where he presented a riveting program at a large insurance group's risk management

conference, and I presented a program on Armed Intruder/ Active Shooter with a colleague. Of the several hundred attendees at the workshop, scores and scores of them greeted Frank after his program with smiles, hugs, and tears, telling him how inspirational he was.

*—**Stan Szpytek**, President,*
Fire and Life-Safety, Inc

Frank DeAngelis is a national treasure who has trans-formed the school safety conversation worldwide. His honesty and unwavering commitment that those lost in our Columbine tragedy will never be forgotten is reflected in a willingness to share the difficult lessons learned and his own very moving and personal journey.

I have worked with Frank for more than a decade during unimaginable crisis events in our District, including the Deer Creek Middle School shooting and the kidnapping and murder of ten-year-old Jessica Ridgeway as well as several credible threats to Columbine High School. Frank's genuine compas-sion and ability to connect with students, parents, educators, and first responders is inspirational and a significant reason we have been able to successfully recover and thrive. Frank didn't just rebuild the climate and culture at Columbine High School, he restored the faith of our entire community.

*—**John McDonald**,*
Security and Emergency Management,
Jeffco Public Schools

That man, John McDonald, has set a standard of excellence in school safety. His long-standing ties to the Columbine commu-nity and understanding of the lessons learned from the Columbine tragedy led to one of the most innovative and effective ideas in the industry.

In 2014, McDonald approached Jeffco Schools' Chief Operating Officer, Steve Bell, a former Wheat High School teacher and coach, proposing to repurpose an elementary school that was closed in 2011 and convert it to a first-responder training center. His intent was to provide a center where the lessons learned from mass shootings happening around the country could be discussed and used to create specialized training curriculum and simulations. The idea was to provide a place where egos were checked at the door, and effective tactics were developed and practiced. McDonald wanted to provide a center that would allow law enforcement, fire fighters, and paramedics a place to train for mass casualty events anywhere in the community.

On April 19, 2017, McDonald and Jeffco Schools dedicated the training facility. I didn't know it, but they arranged for my entire family to be present as they renamed the former grade school The Frank DeAngelis Center for Community Safety.

In August 2017, Congresswoman Diana DeGette met McDonald, Bell, Jeffco Superintendent Dr. Jason Glass, school board members Ron Mitchell and Amanda Stevens, me, and others at the center for a tour and demonstration, and we all watched as officers from Commerce City performed training in simulations in the hallways.

As I write in late 2018, the center has already been booked for more than 195 days by forty-six local, state, and federal agencies. SWAT teams, bomb squads, school resource officers, patrol, and K-9 units are all training at the center. To date, more than five thousand first responders have worked to learn tactics that will save lives. From tactical casualty care to rapid and immediate deployment, single-officer response to crime scene investigations, and Navy Seal training, this former school continues to be a place of education, albeit with a different kind of teacher and student.

In addition to this training center, there are a number of positive groups and organizations that have come out of tragic events. What follows are a few of the remarkable people and foundations with which I've had the honor to partner:

koshkafoundation.org

Kristina Anderson, a survivor of the 2007 Virginia Tech school shooting, started the Koshka Foundation for Safe Schools. The foundation's mission is to "increase public awareness, training, and education towards violence prevention through threat assessment and management, helping individuals create active threat response plans, and post-crisis recovery planning within schools, workplaces, and public spaces."

safeandsoundschools.org

Michele Gay and Alissa Parker, whose daughters Josephine and Emile were killed at Sandy Hook, started the Safe and Sound Schools Foundation. Their mission is "to support school crisis prevention, response, and recovery, and to protect every school and every student, every day." Safe and Sound Schools has maintained an unwavering focus on school safety. Michele, the executive director and a former teacher, has gathered and developed the research-based education, tools, and resources they provide to schools at no cost to ensure the safety of schools across the country, in memory of her daughter.

guard911.com/blog

Nate McVicker is a veteran police officer and founder of Guard911. That company's SchoolGuard service places a "Panic Button" in the hands of all approved staff members with a smartphone app. The app empowers the staff member to immediately call 911. It also immediately notifies all other teachers and nearby properties of a threat and contacts all federal and local law-enforcement personnel in close proximity. Those officers have a law enforcement-exclusive "app," Hero911, that works with Guard911.

iloveuguys.org

The Keyes family and their I Love U Guys Foundation promote school safety. I've already mentioned them, but it's appropriate to do it again here. I Love U Guys Foundation promotes school safety. In 2009, the Foundation collaborated with schools and first responders to create the Standard Response Protocol and began an outreach program to show schools and first responders how it works. The results have been simply astonishing. It has reached millions of students, hundreds of thousands of educators, administrators, and school staff and tens of thousands of first responders. All are using the same language and have the same training expectations of behavior during a crisis. In 2012, research indicated there was another gap in the spectrum of school safety. Few schools had a plan to reunify students with parents after a crisis while maintaining accountability and accommodating mental health demands. Again, collaboration and research resulted in the Standard Reunification Method.

Today the foundation offers trainings, presentations, and materials on the SRP and SRM for school districts, law enforcement, first responders, businesses, and colleges.

chsaf.org

In retirement, I also am involved with several other charities not connected to the school safety effort. One of them, of course, is the Frank DeAngelis Columbine High School Academic Foundation. Yes, the challenge of properly funding public education remains.

columbinememorial.org

The Columbine Memorial Foundation's committee was charged with developing a consensus recommendation to create a physical, permanent memorial for our community and others to honor and respect those touched by the Columbine tragedy. Through the planning process, the Columbine Memorial Committee, representing the Columbine community, envisioned the Columbine Memorial to be a place of remembrance, peace, and spirituality. The memorial would serve to provide comfort and hope for the community at large. The Columbine Memorial foundation's purpose is to augment and facilitate maintenance, repairs, and improvements to the Columbine Memorial. The foundation also coordinates volunteer groups throughout the year to perform trash removal, weeding, plant maintenance, and general cleaning of the Memorial.

carusofamilycharities.org

Caruso Family Charities, the brainchild of my long-time friend Jerry Caruso, supports families whose children are being treated in Colorado for life-threatening diseases. Caruso Family Charities is a 501(c)3 non-profit organization dedicated to assisting families who have a child, adolescent or young adult being treated in Colorado for a life-threatening disease or life-altering event. Through their Funding Families program, the mission is to relieve some financial pressures, such as rent, insurance payments, energy bills, co-pays, or gas so the family may focus on caring for their sick child.

bigideaproject.org

The Big Idea Project is a turn-key program that started at Columbine under the leadership of teacher Bryan Halsey, developing the curriculum to promote leadership in high school students. The project has spread to many other Colorado high schools.

upliftinternationale.org

Through its Operation Taghoy, Uplift Internationale supports mission trips of medical personnel and community leaders to the Philippines, where the physicians operate on poor children with facial deformities.

shilohhouse.org

Shiloh House, with several centers in the Denver area, is a non-profit organization that provides both residential and non-residential treatment to young people who have been subjected to abuse, neglect, and trauma.

hylandhillsfoundation.org

The Hyland Hills Foundation's mission is to promote and support the recreational and cultural opportunities of Hyland Hills residents. The Foundation is a 100 percent volunteer-run organization designed to provide assistance to the citizens of the Hyland Hills Parks and Recreation District community, particularly children. A small group of concerned citizens formed it as a nonprofit corporation in October 1992. The goal of the foundation then and now is to assist the Hyland Hills Parks and Recreation District in providing the very best recreational facilities to all, regardless of financial ability to pay or background.

I encourage anyone interested in additional information on any of those organizations, including how to donate to the charities, to please visit the websites.

Also in retirement, I am a doting grandfather and husband.

Diane DeAngelis

66 *When Frank came back into my life, my kids, Nicole and Matt, were a big part of my life. As so many others have, they have grown to love and respect Frank. They know he has made*

a huge difference in my life and theirs. We are blessed to have a five-year-old granddaughter, Mia Isabella, in our lives. Mia loves her Papa Frank. She has both of us wrapped around her little finger. We are blessed to be husband and wife and to have two great kids, Nicole and Matt, and we cherish being grandparents for our adorable Mia. We look forward to growing old together. 🙶

I am blessed to have Nicole and Matt accept me into their lives. I am proud for what they have accomplished. Nicole is a nurse, and Matt is a firefighter. Each day they are helping others and have a special place in my heart. As Diane often notes, Mia is the "apple of my eye." I always look forward to spending time with her when I return from my trips. Her smile and hugs brighten even the darkest days.

Exercising discretion, I found several ways to stay involved with Columbine after officially leaving the school. I didn't want to be perceived as hovering or meddling as my successor, Dr. KC Somers, did terrific work and continued the tradition of leadership set by Gerry Difford, Terry Conley, Warren Hanks, and Ron Mitchell before me. (All four of them had their own styles, and each had a positive impact on my life. I came to Columbine after Difford left to pursue other educational opportunities, but he was always there whenever I needed help or advice.) I often joke that when Dr. Somers was hired, they had upgraded, finding someone taller and smarter. I greatly appreciate Dr. Somers allowing me to stay involved. He invited me back to participate at assemblies, graduations, and other activities. He welcomed me back to the school on April 20 each year and for the annual Run for Remembrance. Proceeds from the run go to the Frank DeAngelis Academic Fund, The Columbine Permanent Memorial Foundation, and Craig Hospital.

When I had the pleasure of introducing KC to the Columbine staff as their new principal, I noted that I was taking the Olympic Torch that hung on my office wall with me (because if times get difficult financially during my retirement, I may have to sell it on eBay), so when I said I was passing on the torch of this school's leadership to the very capable Dr. Somers, I didn't mean it literally. My assistant principal, Scott Christy, succeeded Dr. Somers in the fall of 2017. Scott has welcomed me back with open arms. I will help him as the Columbine School Community plans for the twentieth anniversary in 2019. I greatly enjoy serving as a mentor for Scott, and his outstanding leadership will provide the students and staff the opportunity to continue to stretch for excellence. He makes me realize that I am a Rebel for life, and I am grateful to him and the members of the staff who greet me with smiles and hugs when I visit Columbine. The future is bright under the leadership of Mr. Christy. That was the agenda Dr. Difford started back in 1973.

Tim Capra, our special education teacher and golf coach, loved to joke that in our nineteen years together, I tried to fire him nineteen times, but we always worked it out. Eventually he lasted two years longer than I did, retiring in 2016. In the fall after I left the principal's job, I served as Tim's assistant boys' golf coach for two years. I had to overcome Tim's friendly skepticism because one of his pastimes was to make fun of my golf game.

"Have you ever seen Frank play golf?" he would ask others.

If they said no, he would say, "You don't want to."

Finally, we agreed on what my role would be.

Tim called me his motivation coach. Whenever a player was struggling, I'd deliver a pep talk. "It was right in Frank's wheelhouse," Tim said later. I had a great time in the fall of 2015 and 2016 before I stepped away.

Retirement also gave me time to attend our monthly birthday lunches and our annual Christmas party with Rocky Carbone, Ricky DeBell, Jerry Caruso, John Wasinger, Mike Bucci, Jimmy Ruscetta, Steve Pacifico, Tony DiTirro, Derald Bellio, Mike Bellio, Danny Martinelli, Johnny Sannino, Steve Egender, Steve LaBriola, Steve Johnson, Tony Cito, and my dad and brother. At times it reminds me of scenes from *The Godfather*. I have a great circle of friends, ones I can count on to support me. Each month, I try to attend the Mount Carmel Men's Club meeting, an evening of great food and great stories, but more importantly, time spent with great friends.

Each summer I get to work at the Mount Carmel Bazaar with the friends whom I grew up with and admired. I mentioned some of them earlier, and there are many others, including Jackie Caruso, John Caruso, John Capone, Fred Marzano, Rusty Parisi, Phil Rossi, Bobby Campbell, Ernie Marranzino, Jerry Petrocco, Paulie Garrimone, John Dezzutti, Glenn Churchill, Scott Nelson, Hank Fanelli, Chuck Bur, Louie Buccino, Bob Kockevar, Bob D'Ascoli, Bobby Quintana, Steve, Rondinelli, Mike Rondinelli, John Incampo, Tommy Ligrani, George Masciotro, Jerry and Steve Smaldone, Don Stevenson, Mike Volpe, Jimmy Vecchiarelli, and Mike Pomponio. I cannot state it enough: My childhood friends and experiences helped make me who I am, and even fifty years later, I know I can always count on their support and friendship.

A few years ago, I was invited by Regis Jesuit High School President Rick Sullivan to do a back-to-school presentation at the school in suburban Parker, Colorado. It was a bit of a culture shock for me because, when I was being raised, Regis High School was located in North Denver on the same grounds as Regis University. I had many friends who attended Regis High, especially after Mt. Carmel closed my freshmen year. Among those classmates and teammates who went to Regis High were Rick Carollo, Jerry

Caruso, and Edgie Walrath. So when Rick Sullivan asked me to speak to the members of the men and women's staff at Regis, I was honored. It was a special day. I spotted a few friends Steve Cavnar, Glenn Churchill, and Charlie Saulino in the auditorium. Charlie and I had served together as altar boys at Mount Carmel. He now is six-foot-six. I am not. Even in our childhoods, he was considerably taller, and we received a lot of strange looks from the members of the congregation. He would kneel and I could stand, and he would still be taller than me. Charlie both taught and was the principal at Regis, so it made the day even more special. He recently retired after spending forty years at the high school.

My faith, which has been subjected to so many tests, remains undiminished. After I retired, John Bandimere Jr.—who owns Bandimere Speedway in Morrison, just outside Denver—invited me to join a Bible study group he had started. We meet at 6:15 on Monday mornings, so it is for early risers. Among those who also joined Bandimere were buddy Jerry Caruso, long-time Colorado Rockies radio broadcaster Jerry Schemmel (whose children attended Columbine), Larry Wickes, Darren Hensely, Chris Hernandez, Mark Neely, Jim Rada, John Scott, Jeff Seltz, John Gallo, Rick Roberts, Joe Spelic, and Ken Webb.

In addition, I occasionally attend a Bible study group of Columbine teachers and coaches and Front Ranch teachers and coaches. Brad Widstrom continues to lead the group; it was Gary Fuller who brought us together after the tragedy. The group was a great spiritual support for me during my career, and it continues to encourage me in my retirement. Now more than ever before, I realize that I would not made it through the years since 1999 were it not for my faith.

I still annually invite the families of the murdered, the families of the injured, and the injured themselves to come to Columbine on April 20, and I call the families of the murdered to tell them that they are in my thoughts and prayers and always will be. Each day, I recite the names of my Beloved Thirteen, and I will not allow them to be forgotten.

I keep thinking of the cheer, "We are . . . Columbine." In retirement I'm trying to emphasize that we are *all* Columbine. Yes, even in a world in which school shootings and other mass killings take place with numbing regularity, we're *all* Columbine.

I will continue to fight the good fight to seek to help eliminate the violent acts of terrorism that continue to take our children's lives. We continue to mourn the senseless deaths that occur at schools around the world. But we don't hear about plans thwarted, because of lessons learned from Columbine.

The one thing I can say, whether it was teaching, coaching, or being a principal, is that I gave it my best.

I'm retired; I'm not done.

Chapter Twenty

Leadership

The Golden Rule was my standard, thanks to my parents. I never, not once, demanded respect from students or staff members because I was the principal. If I were doing my job the right way, that respect would come—because I had earned it. Being a good leader wasn't necessarily about being popular, but about being respected. Staff members learned that I truly meant it when I said I wanted and would consider everyone's opinion, even if I ultimately disagreed. If they walked out mad about my decision, okay, but I believe they never felt as if they had been ignored or patronized.

I try to heed the advice of motivational speaker and self-development author Brian Tracy: "Become the kind of leader that people would follow voluntarily even if you had no title or position."

You treat people the way you want to be treated. The way you deal with people matters, but that doesn't mean you have to be a pushover. No one wants to be yelled at in front of their colleagues or peers. Ridiculing kids in front of other kids or staff members in front of other staff members isn't the way to create the climate we need in schools. I have come to prefer, and cite, the Winston Churchill quote: "Tact is the ability to tell someone to go to hell in such a way that they look forward to the trip."

I led with my heart. Even when I had to discipline teachers or kids, they still knew I cared about them.

After the Columbine tragedy, I was at a point in my life where I couldn't dwell on the negative. I had to build on the positive. Unfortunately, it seems leaders spend about 95 percent of their time dealing with 5 percent of the people who are negative. To me, that's wasted energy. I look for people who are energy givers, not energy takers.

I've adopted the following definition of the difference between a "Boss" and a "Leader":

BOSS	LEADER
Demands	Coaches
Relies on Authority	Relies on Goodwill
Issues Ultimatums	Generates Enthusiasm
Says, "I"	Says, "We"
Uses People	Develops People
Takes Credit	Gives Credit
Places the Blame	Accepts the Blame
Says, "Go."	Says, "Let's Go."
My Way is the Only Way	Strength in Unity

In my final year as principal, a teacher told me, "You were not an administrator; you were an educator." That was true from Day 1 for me on the job as principal. I considered it important to nurture leadership throughout the school, and I delegated rather than micromanaged. The final decisions were mine, but the process was collaborative. I emphasized the concept of working as a team, and I made sure to share the credit for our efforts.

I know there are a lot of executives—even in education— whose leadership style revolves around instilling fear in their followers. I don't know how far that gets you. For me, I never had to tell a staff member, "You will do it because I'm your boss." I never told a kid, "You will do it because I'm the principal." There were times I had to suspend kids for their actions, but they knew I cared about them. I would call them when they were suspended, and when they came back, I would make sure they were doing all right.

What I found out over the years is that it's more effective to say something like, "I need a favor: I need you to carry out this project, and if you need help, I'm here," as opposed to saying, "I want you to carry out this project," and then hovering over that person every step of the way.

As an administrator, if I told the members of the staff, "This is what we need to do," they were thinking that was what I wanted them to do; however, if while working with department leaders to come up with a plan the teachers shared the plan with staff members, they realized it was a team decision. I tried to encourage department leaders to do the same. I'd want to make sure they were getting input from the members of their department, in part because when people are involved in any decision or project, they have ownership of its success.

I encouraged all, not just the most vocal, to contribute. As I gained experience as principal, department leaders came to me. When I assumed they were representing the members of their department, it often was a mistake. I learned in some instances they were representing a hidden agenda of their own and weren't representing their colleagues. That's why communication is so important. Leaders need to check in with people who might disagree with them. Doing so will give you a real climate check for your organization. Too many times, we search for the people who tell us what we want to hear. Their words may make us feel good, but that tactic will not provide an accurate account of the school climate.

Being a good listener is essential to effective leadership. For myself as a guy, I know that men have the tendency to want to fix things. If you are married, maybe you can relate to this: My wife, Diane tells me about something she's struggling with, and within two minutes, I start to tell her what needs to be done. Then she starts yelling at me, and I respond with "I was just trying to help!" Her response: "I don't need your help, I just need you to listen."

Leaders, male or female, sometimes make the same mistake. Staff members come into our offices and might just need to talk and have someone listen. But we immediately tell them what they should do or how they should feel. It's paramount to listen first. Once they ask for advice or want our opinion, that's the time to offer suggestions. Until then, just listen. What you'll find many times is that in doing so, you empower your people to find the solution to their problems.

In January 2016, I taught a two-day graduate class at Soka University in Laguna Beach, and six students were working toward their master's in a leadership program. One of the students, Jamie Haynes, mentioned that I brought up recurring themes and put together a list of "Mr. De's Bes: Leadership Tips." I believe that the advice is not only good for leaders of organizations but also can be used in all areas of our lives. For parents, this can be helpful.

Be Visible

I was not an office principal. The thing I did not like about being an administrator was the number of meetings to attend or being out of Columbine High School. It was a tough decision leaving the classroom to become an administrator. I was afraid I was going to lose touch with the students. I made a promise to spend time in the classrooms every day. I loved lunchroom duty because

I could converse with the students informally; I loved being in the hallway during passing periods and before and after school. It saddens me when students who attended other schools tell me they seldom saw their principals. Visibility was so important after the tragedy; the students and staff needed to see me, and I needed to be with them.

Be Honest

Honesty was instilled in me by my parents and members of my family. Instilling trust is a key component to a successful organization. It is paramount to creating an environment that values honesty. Not only what you say is important, but what you do is equally so. One of my favorite quotes is this one from C.S. Lewis: "Integrity is doing the right thing even when no one is watching." People want the truth even if it is not what they want to hear. I have always worn my emotions on my sleeve. I was never accused of having a "Poker Face."

Be Empathetic

It's important to understand where people are coming from. Many times we believe we know how someone is feeling. But do we take the time to find out more? Rarely. Our feelings may not be in line with their feelings. We initially assumed students were lazy or didn't care about school, because they didn't turn in homework or come to class. When that happened, I advised staff members to dig deeper; for example, could it be that students weren't turning in homework because they were reading below their grade level? Or could it be they were missing school because they had to work to support their family? It's not always as simple as it seems. In dealing with students, we lose credibility when we make assumptions and do not take the time and effort to find out what is actually going on in their lives.

Be Flexible

When situations are out of our control, flexibility allows an organization to be successful. I became a better leader when I found different ways to come up with a solution or accomplish a goal. After the Columbine tragedy, flexibility became a way of life. It was so difficult because I had little control on many things. I could have the best plan, and an event would happen, and we'd have to modify and change our plan or come up with a new strategy. Being flexible and being able to "think on your feet" are essential.

Be a Good Listener

Communication is the key to success within an organization. You cannot communicate enough. I learned that from our superintendent, Dr. Cindy Stevenson. Others feel valued when they have input and you listen. Too often, leaders tend to do all the talking and do very little listening. As a leader, ultimately you are responsible for making the final decision. But listening helps in making decisions. It is essential to get input from those who don't agree with you. I often listened to people who gave me information I didn't want to hear, but it was what I needed to hear. As a principal, it is important to listen to all students, not just the student leaders.

Be Generous Assigning Credit

The success of an organization requires setting goals and having a plan to meet the goals. It is important to establish guidelines that you assess to make sure you are on the right track, then make modifications whenever necessary. Once the goals are set and an organization meets each one, it's important to make clear it was a team effort. Assigning credit is important. As a leader, if you feel you are the smartest in the organization and that the organization cannot function without your presence, and you do not listen to others in the organization, you limit the capability of the organization to grow. You're not utilizing all the available knowledge.

I have witnessed organizations in which leaders have sabotaged or set their co-workers up to fail. Why? To make sure everyone knows the leader is the most important and smartest person in the organization. I have seen instances of leaders not sharing their knowledge, thinking if they are the only ones who know what to do, it will enhance their job security. That's a grave mistake because you will never build the leadership capacity in the organization. You will not develop a team. At Columbine, we were 150 strong as a staff, and all contributed to our success. Columbine is a great school. It's not because of the bricks and mortar but because of the people who walk the halls—students, staff members, and parents. I could not have been a successful leader if I hadn't had a great team. We are Columbine!

Be Careful in Making Generalizations

Often, perceptions are not reality. Assumptions might not be accurate. We make generalizations that do not represent the entire organization. We tend to make statements that might represent a small percentage of an organization. Early in my career, some tried to make it easy, telling me that this was how everyone felt. I made decisions based upon the generalization. That was a grave mistake. The generalization was wrong. In truth, some felt that way. I soon realized they were not representing everyone. I became a better leader when I talked to others within our school to see if the sentiments being represented were the true feelings of the larger population.

Be a Heart-Led Leader

This was one of my strengths as a leader. I led with my heart. When asked what type of leader I was before the tragedy, I said I was the same type of leader I was after the tragedy. I led with my heart whether it was as a teacher, coach, senate sponsor, assistant principal, or principal. It's about developing positive relationships.

It's caring about people and sharing your heart with people. Yes, there are times you become vulnerable when you open up. As a leader, you have to feel comfortable being who you are. I led with heart because of my parents and family members. A colleague told me students can sniff out a phony in seconds. You must be true to yourself before you can be true to others.

Be Inclusive

Creating an environment in which everyone feels welcome is a monumental task but essential to creating a successful organization. As I've noted, we have a tendency to only solicit comments from people who will tell us what we want to hear. In a large school such as Columbine, it was important that I communicated with students who didn't have the best grades, or weren't athletes, or weren't in band. I became a better principal when I sought input from as many students as possible to make sure they felt they were members of our family. I challenged students and staff to make everyone feel welcome. The larger the organization, the more difficult is the task. But it can be done.

Here's just one example of how we worked to increase connection and inclusion at Columbine: The members of our counseling department brought in a program sponsored by MTV. Students were referred by staff members to attend the one-day program. An activity that helped in creating a more inclusive environment was called "Crossing the Line." We had a diverse population in attendance. When they first entered that gymnasium, participants had their own perception of the others there. There were students who were perceived to have everything going for them and other students who struggled. The students often didn't take the time to find out about schoolmates who didn't share their interests. Perceptions were formed because of clothing, hair color, or cars they drove. Then perceptions would change as the students interacted. The facilitator had students and staff members stand on one side of the half-court line in the gymnasium, then started asking questions. How many of you have ever been verbally abused by a parent or loved one? Seventy-five percent of the students crossed the line, signifying their answer was yes. Students who hadn't communicated with many of the others participating in the activity realized others faced the same challenges. How many of you have grown up in a household where alcohol or drugs have been abused? Again, many crossed the line. After more questions, students soon realized they had more in common than they had believed when they walked into the gymnasium. Tears and hugs followed. This was a great activity for changing the culture of a school and stressing the point that perception is not necessarily reality.

Love, Love, Love

Love. Enough said!

I've done considerable reading about leadership and learned a lot about it from several authors. I took to heart what Liz Wiseman wrote in her book *Multipliers*. She mentions two types of leaders: "Diminishers" and "Multipliers." She writes that Diminishers are absorbed in their own intelligence, stifle others, and deplete the organization of crucial intelligence and capability. Then she adds that Multipliers are genius makers. They bring out the intelligence in others and build collective viral intelligence in organizations. She expands on that, adding in great detail to the definitions of the "Multipliers" and "Diminishers."

Other books that have influenced me are *Greater Than Yourself* and *The Radical Leap Re-Energized*, by Steve Farber, and two from Tommy Spaulding, *The Heart-Led Leader* and *It's Not Just Who You Know*. (Yes, there is a chapter about me in the former.) Steve and Tommy have been great mentors for me. Each June, Spaulding gives me the opportunity to present to high school students from around the country at his National Leadership Academy in Colorado, and Farber invited me to speak at his Extreme Leadership Conference in Chicago.

I've met a lot of prominent leaders over the years, and one of the most memorable discussions I've had was with Rudy Giuliani. Along with a few other community leaders, Diane and I were invited to a sit-down dinner with Giuliani when he was making speaking engagements in Colorado. I spent two hours with him, and he talked about leadership. When he was discussing how he dealt with 9/11 as the mayor of New York, it made me think of the way I dealt with our situation at Columbine. I'm not comparing myself with Giuliani, but I was nodding my head a lot. He wears his emotions on his sleeve. He ended up trying to go to as many memorial services of the fallen 9/11 officers as possible, and he also was asked by daughters whose fathers had been killed in the Twin Towers to walk them down the aisle. What I gained from him was an affirmation of what I felt about compassion and empathy. Several years later, when United Way invited me to Sandy Hook in February 2013, Mayor Giuliani was the keynote speaker at the function. I was sitting with many of the faculty members at Sandy Hook when the event was about to start. Someone tapped me on the shoulder and asked me to follow him to a room, where Mayor Giuliani was waiting before going on stage. I didn't think he would ever remember me, but he gave me a big bear hug. We had an opportunity to catch up on what we had been doing since the last time we were together. I asked him for a favor. I knew it would be important if the Sandy Hook staff members could have a picture taken with Mayor Giuliani. He graciously posed with them.

So many leaders and authors have impacted my thinking on leadership. But when I close my presentations, I always point to the memorable speech made by Martin Luther King Jr., and ask, "What is your dream?"

My dream is that the events of April 20, 1999, had never happened.

But because they did, my dream is that we will all move forward with wisdom and love and make the most of the future. We will always remember our Beloved Thirteen, and all students and staff members who have lost their lives or have been injured because of acts of violence.

Chapter Twenty-One

Gun Rights . . . and Wrongs

Every public or mass shooting inevitably restarts the debate over gun control. That was true with Columbine, and it was true after the horrific events in Las Vegas on October 1, 2017, when a single shooter with an arsenal in his thirty-second-floor room at the Mandalay Bay Hotel fired down into a country music festival crowd, killing fifty-eight and wounding many more. It became a heated topic after the Marjory Stoneman Douglas High School shootings on February 14, 2018. The students at the school took their concerns nationwide, calling for action with national leaders.

At Columbine, the killers had a TEC-DC 9 semi-automatic handgun, a 9mm carbine, a sawed-off 12-gauge pump shotgun, and a sawed-off double-barreled shotgun. They did the sawing off themselves, making the guns easier to conceal but more difficult to shoot accurately.

Neither Harris nor Klebold were eighteen in November 1998 when they attended the Tanner Gun Show, which was held almost every month at the Denver Merchandise Mart in Adams County, just beyond the Denver city limits. There they scouted out possible purchases, then returned the next day with Klebold's friend and later his prom date, Robyn Anderson, an excellent student and nice girl active in church organizations. She had just turned eighteen, which made her old enough to purchase guns.

Dealers at the show were both federally licensed and unlicensed. Unlicensed meant relatively unregulated, with less paperwork and scrutiny. All that I've read leads me to believe that it was obvious that Anderson was buying for Harris and Klebold, who were with her. But with a driver's license that showed she was eighteen, she was the official and legal purchaser of the carbine and the two shotguns from three different private, unlicensed dealers. Anderson paid cash—the killers' cash—and she later said she didn't have to fill out anything, and there were no receipts involved.

Under Colorado law, an eighteen-year-old without a felony record could legally furnish minors with "long guns" (i.e., rifles and shotguns). Federal laws about "straw" shotgun and rifle sales—sales in which others purchase guns for minors—and sales to minors were tighter, but only applied to licensed dealers.

After the killings, a horrified Anderson told her mother about the gun purchases, and her mother took her to the school, where the Columbine Task Force had set up in the band room. She was questioned for four hours, but was insistent she had no idea about the killers' plans for the guns. Anderson later said that if she'd had to undergo a background check or fill out extensive paperwork, she would have balked at making the purchases. She was never charged with a crime.

Tom Mauser, the father of the murdered Daniel Mauser, took a one-year leave of absence from his job at the Colorado

Department of Transportation to be a lobbyist for an organization proposing stricter gun control laws in Colorado. When the legislature wasn't very responsive, and the few bills that did passed were weak, Mauser's organization led the successful petition drive to get Amendment 22 on the November 2000 ballot. The initiative, billed as closing the gun-show loophole, passed decisively, requiring background checks for buyers of firearms at gun shows. The state also required all transactions at the shows to go through licensed dealers. Then in 2013, Colorado began requiring even unlicensed sellers to run background checks on buyers in all transactions, not just at shows. The only exception was for antique guns.

If those laws had been in effect in 1998 and 1999, perhaps the killers would have managed to acquire three "long guns," anyway. But they would have had to go about it differently and might have drawn attention to themselves.

The handgun, the TEC-DC 9, came from Mark Manes, introduced to Harris and Klebold by their fellow Blackjack Pizza employee Philip Duran. Manes sold the killers the gun, which he had purchased at an earlier Tanner show, for $500. On the Basement Tapes, the killers thanked Manes for helping them acquire the TEC-DC9, used by Klebold on April 20, 1999. The tapes also showed them talking about trying out the gun, shooting at a tree and chortling about what the gun could do to a victim. Both Manes and Duran eventually were charged with selling a handgun—as opposed to a "long gun"—to minors and served prison time.

To the disappointment of some, I am not a militant absolutist on gun control, primarily because I believe banning all guns won't get much done. I believe it is one piece to the puzzle. Other pieces are mental health, background checks, the role that social media plays, parenting, plus law enforcement and judicial systems working together with schools.

I have friends who strongly believe in the right to bear arms and who oppose significant gun control legislation, saying the problem is with society, not with guns. I realize that people who intend to commit murder will purchase weapons illegally, if necessary. Chicago has some of the toughest gun laws in the country and has the highest homicide rate. I know that supporters of tougher gun laws argue that the guns being used in Chicago are being purchased in states where their laws are more lax and being brought into Chicago. I respect the gun rights advocates' right to their opinion. Law-abiding citizens do whatever they need to do to follow the laws.

How do you stop the excesses in a society where it's made easy for guns to be purchased illegally, and where it still isn't hard enough to purchase guns legally?

That's where I struggle.

I believe there should be some middle ground that helps lessen the chances of mass killings, and reasonable measures such as those championed by Tom Mauser are praiseworthy steps in the right direction. I can't reconcile the idea of an eighteen-year-old girl buying guns that have no productive use in society. Ultimately, these guns were used for their intended purpose, to kill and wound. Yes, there's something wrong with laws that allow that to happen.

Loopholes still exist, and they need to be closed. And it's hard for me to imagine why anyone would need a thirty-round magazine for self-protection.

(Answer: Nobody does.)

I do believe that common sense needs to be used by both sides.

I don't agree with the premise that everyone should own a gun, but it is an individual right. A majority of gun owners are law-abiding citizens. I don't believe teachers or administrators should be armed or have access to guns. I wonder how many educators would choose the profession knowing there is the possibility that they would be required to be armed.

That said, I do realize there are extenuating circumstances. During one panel I served on, I shared my opinion about arming teachers. The panelist that followed me lived in a rural area, and he noted it would take an inordinate amount of time for officers to respond there. He said they did have staff members who were armed, but added they were former military or ex-police officers. I have had the good fortune to work with law enforcement officers, and I have not found many who support arming teachers. A concern they have is that once anyone armed enters a building, adults trying to protect the students usually can't be certain they've got the potential shooters spotted. Plus, with very few exceptions, staff members aren't likely to fire with accuracy. I realize if laws ever are passed that would allow teachers and administrators to carry guns, there would have to be stringent guidelines to allow school personnel to carry.

School resource officers are the better choice for enhancing school security. I'm a major supporter of armed school resource officers, assigned from area police or sheriff forces. Mo Canady, the executive director of The National Association of School Resource Officers (NASRO) argues that a well-founded school resource officer (SRO) program is one of the best possible school security investments for any community. The return on that investment, however, goes well beyond school security. NASRO strongly recommends that every school in America have at least one carefully selected, specially trained SRO as opposed to arming teachers. Deputy Blaine Gaskill of the St. Mary's County Sheriff's Office provides an example of the impact an SRO can have. When a school shooting erupted at Great Mills High School in March 2018, Deputy Gaskill responded directly to the threat and stopped the shooting. For this act of courage, Deputy Gaskill received NASRO's 2018 National Award of Valor.

NASRO recommends a triad approach to school policing in which every SRO serves the school community as (1) a mentor/ informal counselor, (2) an educator/guest lecturer, and (3) a law enforcement officer. The former two roles assist the latter role. Developing positive relationships with students enables SROs to gather valuable information that helps them intervene quickly.

I've talked to police officers about what might have happened if I'd had a gun on me that day, whether that meant I always carried one or that I could get to one quickly in my office at the report of gunfire. When I ran out of my office and saw Harris, who knows what I would have done if I'd spotted him sooner and he was closer? (Remember, at that point, we didn't know they had started their killing spree elsewhere. They could have been shooting up the school, not committing murder.) I would have said, "Come on, there has to be a better way; put the gun down." I saw the gunman as one of my students. We can't break down the possibilities second by second, but I believe that if I had been carrying a gun and Harris had seen that, he might have reacted differently, whether before or after his initial blast in my direction.

I also know that I could go out every week to a firing range and perfect my aim. But it's the mental piece that makes me question the wisdom of being armed: Would I be able to kill someone? Would I have hesitated to shoot? Probably. And the officers I've spoken with agree that if I'd had a gun and didn't fire it, Harris would have killed me and the girls that day.

Police officers say that when they run into a building, they see the perpetrator. They see a threat to others. They react. When an officer shoots, he or she isn't aiming for the leg. He or she is doing everything possible to stop the perpetrator(s) from killing innocent children.

Again, I am not against law-abiding citizens owning guns. But I think we do need to look at both sides. Jaclyn Schildkraut, a professor at Oswego University, and H. Jaymi Elsass did extensive research and wrote the book, *Mass Shootings: Media, Myths, and Realities*. Jaclyn later went on to publish. *Mass Shootings in America: Understanding the Debates, Causes, and Responses*. The books present arguments for the never-ending debate. It's safe to say there aren't guarantees that one thing can stop the mass shootings from occurring.

Here's another debate: Do violent video games or violence-themed music motivate potential mass killers? Good question; I don't have a definitive answer.

We must continue the fight to come up with plans and laws that have the potential to stop the senseless murders. At my presentations, audience members often say something like, "Frank it is admirable what you are doing, but school shootings continue." My response is that they're right, but I then ask how many shooting plots have been foiled and how many lives have been saved because of lessons learned and things being done differently after April 20, 1999.

Chapter Twenty-Two

Preventive Measures

In early 1999, experimentation began with a hotline concept. Young people could call and prevent crimes. The idea, initially tested in Colorado Springs, was met with excellent results. The pilot prevention strategy was presented to Colorado's Attorney General Ken Salazar—a former U.S. Secretary of the Interior—and a group of Colorado leaders who recommended replicating the program statewide.

Then the Columbine tragedy occurred. Overnight, school officials had to change the way they thought about their students, school safety, and prevention.

After the shocking events at Columbine, Salazar and Governor Bill Owens commissioned a state-wide study to offer recommendations that could prevent another school massacre. As a direct outcome of the Columbine Commission's Report, the Safe2Tell Initiative was created to implement a critical recommendation: *To provide an anonymous venue for parents, students, teachers, school administrators, and law enforcement to share information.*

In Colorado, policymakers began studying the causes of violence and possible prevention programs. Colorado was already home to one of the most renowned violence prevention centers in the country at the University of Colorado in Boulder. Dr. Del Elliott, Founding Director of the CU-Boulder Center for the Study and Prevention of Violence, spent years studying scientifically proven crime prevention programs. Ken Salazar and Detective Susan Payne worked together on the Safe Communities, Safe Schools initiative. They traveled to every Colorado county on a listening tour, searching for answers to the elusive questions of how to make communities safer.

By 2001, Owens' Columbine Review Commission, which had been studying the Columbine tragedy, released its final report. Among the key findings of the report included an endorsement of Salazar's push for a statewide hotline where anonymous callers could report concerns about potential community violence. The hotline sounded great in theory, but few calls were received in the first few years.

A group of state leaders established the framework for the Safe2Tell model in 2003. The Colorado Trust awarded a seed money grant to develop Safe2Tell Colorado as part of the Crime Stoppers organization. In 2006, the program independently incorporated as a separate 501(c)(3) non-profit organization, and a board of directors was formed. Payne was named executive director of Safe2Tell Colorado and became the first Special Agent with the Colorado Department of Public Safety-Homeland Security to focus on school safety.

Anonymity is key to the success of the Safe2Tell Colorado model. Both state law and the procedures established by Safe2Tell Colorado guaranteed the anonymity of anyone making a report. Calls, web, and mobile app reports are answered at Colorado State Patrol communication centers. When an action is needed, information immediately is forwarded to local school officials and law enforcement agencies. The Safe2Tell Colorado system ensures that each report is investigated by school and law enforcement agencies, that action is taken, and that the outcome is tracked. The assurance that calls are not traced and that appropriate action is taken has established the trust needed to persuade young people to move away from a code of silence and to take a stand. Safe2Tell Colorado has worked to educate and empower young people to keep their community safe.

As the model and use of the reporting resource grew, the need to make the model a state-funded operation became more critical. On May 5, 2014, the Colorado General Assembly adopted Senate Bill 2014-002 (C.R.S. Section 24-31-601 et seq.), incorporating Safe2Tell under the Colorado Office of the Attorney General. Cynthia Coffman took office as attorney general in January 2015 and essentially oversaw Safe2Tell for the next four years, until she returned to private practice in January 2019. That provided the necessary funding to ensure the Safe2Tell Colorado reporting avenues, training, and education and awareness efforts remain available to Colorado students, schools, and communities. In a rare bipartisan effort, Colorado legislators voted unanimously to pass this critical legislation. Safe2Tell now operates as a state-funded program connected to the attorney general's office.

The strategy developed from the Safe2Tell Colorado model prevents tragedy and saves lives. Safe2Tell Colorado works to change attitudes by providing resources around the state to educate, equip, empower, and engage youth. Safe2Tell Colorado works to break the code of silence through awareness, education, and outreach activities. Safe2Tell has grown to be a nationally recognized model of prevention focused on best practices in school safety across the United States.

As I write, I'm hopeful that a national Safe to Tell Act will be enacted. Congressmen Mike Coffman (R-Colorado) and James Himes (D-Connecticut) introduced HR 6713, a measure along those lines. It would provide federal grants to states that established 24/7 systems for anonymous reports to alert law enforcement about potential threats to schools.

Earlier, I gave details of security programs implemented as a result of lessons learned from Columbine. That's part of our legacy too.

Each time another shooting occurs, there are lessons to be gleaned about what was effective and what needs to be done differently. Times have changed. The fire drills of my youth have given way to students and staff members practicing lockdown, evacuation, and reunification drills.

The emergency plans prepare our students and school staff members for the worst, but drills also are taking place at businesses, health care facilities, and churches. That's because we have learned the hard way that no one is immune. As terrorist attacks continue around the world, we must be prepared. We can no longer take the stance that if we don't talk about, it will not happen.

On any given day, the unthinkable can happen.

We must be prepared.

Chapter Twenty-Three

State of Public Education

Late in my career, I noticed a change in the attitude of many parents. I'm not saying they still didn't support the staff members and the teachers. Columbine still was largely a convivial place to teach and work, but it seemed parents couldn't believe their kids could ever do anything wrong.

I worry about these kids as they become adults and what happens when they don't get that job or that promotion, or they don't get accepted into the college they've applied to. You have to love and support your kids, but they need to learn that they will sometimes fail. Failures can teach us, or they can break us if we aren't equipped to rebound. My fear for today's kids is that they haven't been allowed to experience and learn from failure. What I tried to stress to the students is that mistakes are inevitable, but what's most important is to learn to avoid repeating the same mistakes.

Through the years, I've noticed that parents have become more protective; That's not wrong—or right; it is just different from decades past. I can't imagine my father talking to a teacher about a grade or to a coach about little Frankie not getting enough playing time. When I was attending a parochial school, if my parents ever received a phone call from one of the nuns, my parents supported the nuns. I would face the consequences when I got home. I did mention earlier a few instances in my younger years where I made some bad choices, and there were consequences to face not only at school but also when I got home.

I have heard stories that parents are even questioning college professors about their child's grades. I was amazed when someone who works for a college in the parking and transportation department shared with me that parents were calling and yelling at her because their son or daughter had to walk too far to get from his or her parking spot to his or her dorm room. I am not saying that I had to walk two miles to school uphill both ways in the freezing cold, but I am telling you times have changed. (It was only one mile uphill both ways.)

You're going to love your kids no matter what, but they also need to realize there are consequences for their actions and that life is not always easy or fair.

In developing leadership in kids today, it's important to educate them in math, science, and social studies. It's also the responsibility of our educators *and* parents to teach life skills and character traits. That's a major obligation. Calling to complain about grades and parking spaces only teaches children to be entitled. I feel we should learn from our mistakes and try not to make the same mistake twice. If you only learn to rationalize your mistakes, that's not a lesson at all.

I once read that "our kids are facing mountains to climb, and what we want to do as parents or adults is move the mountains instead of giving the kids the skills to climb it." They're going to need the skills at thirty or thirty-five because parents aren't always able to bail out their kids. To be clear, supporting kids isn't the same as bailing them out. But there's a difference between being there for kids and handling life for them.

I was always amazed when parents came to me and said, "Frank, can you tell my daughter she can't wear that to school?" I'd respond with, "You're the parent." To which the answer was, "Well, she might not like me." Well, so what? Being liked isn't a parent's job. Being a *parent* is the job. They have sixteen- or seventeen-year-old friends. What they need are parents who are brave enough to say no.

Testing

My biggest concern now about the state of public education is whether we're over-testing. My belief is, we sure are. Because of the various testing, I'm concerned that teachers are teaching "to" the tests; for example, I know of an entire department of ninth- and tenth-grade teachers who devoted more than a week of class time on a "boot camp" to help kids figure out what the state test wanted from them because it was different from the college-prep curriculum they taught the rest of the year. They explained that the kind of writing required on the state test was very different from any other writing students would do in their lives. If this was the case, why teach the kind of writing used on the test at all? Getting good scores on a specific test is not necessarily the same thing as productive learning. Administrators and teachers want to be held accountable, and they are, but it's not out of line to ask whether the present system is working.

It worries me that teachers lose some of their instructional and intellectual creative ability because there's so much to cover for the tests. I noticed near the end of my career, when I was doing observations, teachers were more concerned about meeting a standard on the rubric. I did not blame them. This is how they are being evaluated. But I observed many of the teachers more than fifty times during their careers, and their creativity seemed to diminish rather than grow. The reality is the time spent on testing takes away from learning time in the classroom. It started with "No Child Left Behind," but I question whether we're better than we were prior to that program.

I recently had a conversation with long-time Columbine English teacher Paula Reed. We spent more than thirty years together at Columbine. We shared offices together because the offices for the members of the English and social studies department were in the same area when we first started teaching. I had many opportunities to observe her classes along with those of many of her colleagues when I became an administrator. Paula shared this with me:

> Almost every secondary English Language Arts curriculum includes a poetry unit where students study poetry and the terms that describe it, like alliteration and figurative language. Of course, I taught these terms and tested kids over them, but my favorite assessment was about appreciation. Did students appreciate poetry as an artistic expression? No test can measure appreciation; instead, I required a response to a poem, a response that could be anything except an essay. Over the years, students have brought in original art, music, short stories, and poems inspired by a poem they studied. One student gave me a scratchboard of a raven as a response to Poe's "The Raven." Years later, that student returned to Columbine as a custodian, and he was so touched to see that I still had that picture. I could never justify the time we spent as a class on this project using the Common Core State Standards or any of the tightly defined research-based best practices that appear in formal evaluation "look-fors," but it got kids engaged in poetry.

The last several years of my principalship, I was the administrator who worked with members of the English department and was responsible for their evaluations. Columbine has excellent teachers. It was outstanding to have dialogue with the members of the department as changes were implemented. I respected their opinions, and I shared their concerns with members of district leadership. Teachers from the other departments shared the same sentiments about the direction public education was headed.

I especially struggle with testing when you don't get the data back in a timely manner. When I was principal during the Colorado Student Assessment Program (CSAP) testing, students would take the test in the spring, and we didn't get the results back until school was ready to start. It's a measurement, perhaps, but it takes so long to know the results. In most cases, that's just the raw score and not the details of what students got right or wrong, I'm not sure that helps performance in the classroom. Some parents rightly question the time being spent on testing and are asking if it's really improving the education in our schools. Many parents have opted to take their children out of testing, despite the fact that schools and school districts have been punished because the students didn't take the test. In some districts, performance pay for teachers is based on test scores. Teachers have no control over whether students opt out, but their chances for merit pay are affected because students who opted out were given a zero score for the purpose of district ratings and comparisons. Those who support that "zero" system argue it prevents teachers or administrators from encouraging students likely to get low scores to opt out. Anything—even a low score—is better than a zero in determining average scores and district ratings. But I have faith in our school system. That wouldn't happen.

Unlike the ACT and SAT college aptitude tests, there isn't a lot of incentive for students to do well on state-mandated tests.

Students aren't rewarded for doing well, and their scores don't come into play in college admissions. I believe tests that are administered to students from grades eight through ten and are aligned to the ACT test are more valuable for when they take the required ACT test their junior year. The PSAT prepares students for the SAT tests. But even with those tests, raw scores on an annual test every year do not tell the whole story. It is vital to measure student growth throughout the year and with methods more purposeful and revealing than tests.

I also question some of the current teacher-evaluation systems. I know the goal is to improve teaching, but the extensive evaluation being conducted may not be getting the intended results. Even worse, it can be counterproductive if teachers make it their primary goal to get good ratings. This is especially true in this age of "pay for performance." When the district school board decided to tie teacher pay to evaluation, teachers shifted their focus from developing and delivering great lessons to submitting documentation of lesson plans and student performance based on that plan. Sure, this probably led to one great lesson plan, but how much time did it take away from developing another great plan, and then another? I know this model works in the business world, but the incentives are different. Business leaders are paying their employees large bonuses for meeting goals. What I witnessed in education is a small stipend for improving the ranking. The time and effort educators were putting forth to provide documentation to support a higher ranking was taking time from them in preparing their lessons. To me it did not seem to be worth the effort, and more importantly, I don't believe it improved classroom instruction.

Don't get me wrong. I believe teachers should be evaluated. Educators should be accountable for the progress of their students. But there are limits, and excessive attention paid to those evaluations can be a problem. The evaluation system being used at the end of my career at times could seem more punitive than constructive. Teachers believed that administrators felt they must nit-pick and come up with something wrong, even for the best classroom instructors. That sets up an adversarial relationship between teachers and administrators. They're too often antagonists rather than colleagues or teammates, working together to educate kids. There should be more to evaluations than checking off a box. We don't appreciate the value of teachers and administrators as professional educators as much as we should. But as part of that, administrators should absolutely be subject to evaluation too.

Education has changed from when I started in 1979. We have more kids coming in with more needs, including those with English as their second language or with learning disabilities. With family situations changing, we've seen an increase in the need for teachers to be adult role models.

Charter Schools vs. Neighborhood Schools

In the public realm, I know a lot of people believe charter schools are the answer. There are great charter schools. I'm all for school choice, but I believe we need to continue to improve neighborhood schools—wherever those neighborhoods are. Local schools, if well supported, have the potential to be a source of pride and draw communities together. When students go to neighborhood schools, rather than traveling to other areas under open enrollment standards in effect (in Colorado or anywhere else), they develop friendships within those neighborhoods. Students who attend schools outside of their neighborhoods might not have the same opportunities to form those kinds of relationships. If we went back to more aggressively emphasizing the neighborhood concept, maybe we wouldn't need the charter schools.

As a teacher and administrator, I witnessed the community support of Columbine. It extended to Columbine Hills Elementary,

Dutch Creek Elementary, Governors Ranch Elementary, Leawood Elementary, Normandy Elementary, and Ken Caryl Middle School. We were *all* Columbine! It was the sense of pride in the Columbine neighborhood schools that helped us in healing.

At Columbine, we looked at the children from the time they entered kindergarten to the time they graduated from Columbine. Our staff members did horizontal planning, including ninth-grade teachers planning ninth-grade curriculum with other ninth-grade teachers and also with tenth-, eleventh-, and twelfth-grade teachers doing the same. But there was also vertical planning. Our staff members planned with the staff members at the elementary and middle schools.

It becomes more difficult when students leave to go to schools not in the articulation areas. In my time at Columbine, we acted as a team to affect kids all the way through their public school years.

Again, choice is good but not the cure-all. If programs are successful at other schools, including charter schools, I believe neighborhood schools should pay attention. They should be flexible and open-minded. They should consider adopting research-based programs that have worked for others. They should jump on anything that can improve schools rather than stubbornly sticking with existing models.

I seldom came across teachers who weren't willing to do what was best for the students. At times, we didn't give the teachers the tools they needed to be successful. At one point, the emphasis was the catchphrase "differentiated learning." We needed to train teachers to do it. Teachers didn't balk, but I found I agreed with what other educators had said: If you are serious about professional learning and training, you need to set aside time. Many times in education, professional development sessions happen at the end of the day or in the middle of the day. I believed that if you really wanted to do it effectively, teachers should be brought in early and trained during the summer. Compensate them and dedicate time when they can concentrate and do not have to worry about preparing lessons for the next day.

Of course, public school funding has always been a concern, and it's terrific when foundations, such as the one named in my honor at Columbine, step up to raise additional money. I agree that simply throwing money at schools is neither wise nor a guarantee of success. But Colorado is at the lower end of public support for education, and I'm not proud of that. If we do put money into education, we need to make sure it goes to programs that are proven to be successful.

We also need to make sure the people who are making decisions about education are getting input from the grass-roots educators about how to improve the process. That sounds simple, but the decision makers, even in administration, and also in the public policy realm, can be surprisingly naïve about what's going on in school now. Now—not last year or last decade. *Now*. Get out there. Look around. Listen. Yes, even politicians need to be sitting in on classes from time to time.

As a principal, it would have been easy for me to forget what it was like to be a teacher, but I tried during my twenty-plus years as an administrator to spend as much time in the classroom as possible observing teachers. I do not think I was ever accused of not remembering what it was like to be a teacher. Conversely, there were times teachers questioned how I handled a particular situation, and so there were a few instances when I had them sit in "my seat" for a few days during their planning times, and they soon had a better understanding of why I made certain decisions. Listening to one another and working together help to build trust and ensure that everyone is on the same page about what students and teachers really need.

A lot of what we do in education now seems to be like a flavor-of-the month approach. We start a process and don't follow through and finish it, and then we go to the next project. We roll out these great programs, and people get excited, but the follow-up is lacking.

And now, as I move deeper into retirement, I'm concerned about drawing the next wave of great teachers and educators into the business. Law enforcement officers and educators are in the same boat. They're being blamed for a lot of things. In today's climate, it's harder and harder to tell young people to go into education. The risks are greater, and the rewards are limited. That said, those who are called to education come for one reason: the kids— the kids and the classroom. That's why they're in it. As I tell educators, you are not going to become rich but when a student tells you that you had an impact on his or her life you cannot put a price tag on knowing you made a difference. If we want to improve education, we have to ensure bureaucracy doesn't outweigh or diminish what happens in the classroom.

TWENTY-FOUR

From the Columbine Memorial

I'll close with the messages composed by the families and carved into the stone at the Columbine Memorial in Clement Park, adjacent to the high school.

CASSIE BERNALL

Age: 18
Junior

Our Cassie had an engaging laugh, beautiful long hair, clear blue eyes and a big warm smile that she generously shared. Her loves were music, snowboarding with her brother Chris, photography, travel and youth group. Seeking to be an obstetrician, she dreamed of bringing new life into this world.

Cassie truly longed to know what heaven would be like and she strived to know the Lord whom she would meet there. Her heart's desire was *"just to live for Christ."* Weeks before her death she expressed her anxiousness to see heaven, stating that she could *"hardly wait to get there."* When asked how we would ever live without her, Cassie simply replied: *"Wouldn't you be happy for me? You know I'd be in a better place!"*

Cassie lost her life because of her belief in God. Although her dreams of ushering in new life tragically ended, her stand continues to encourage many to seek new life through Christ. We miss her immensely, but we know she's in that better place. Phil. 3:10-11

STEVEN CURNOW

Age: 14
Freshman

Steven Curnow, at 14, was a quiet, thoughtful, generous and forgiving young man. He never held a grudge and was quick to offer help, encouragement, forgiveness and friendship to family, classmates, and soccer teammates.

Steve loved reading, watching adventure movies and playing soccer. When Steve realized he was not skillful enough to make the high school soccer team his dream of playing professional soccer was gone, but he never lost his love for the game. He continued to play on his recreational soccer team and was also a referee.

Steve wanted to pursue his dream of becoming a naval aviator. He had found a love of flying during his first plane trip, a family vacation to England. The plane hit some pretty rough turbulence, dropping altitude, tossing side-to-side and shuddering. Talking on the plane suddenly stopped, with many of the passengers becoming white-knuckled and tightening their grips on the arms of the seats. Ten-year-old Steve's reaction was: "*Wow, that was cool; let's do it again!!*"

Steve, you are forever in our hearts. Soar high, and fly straight. We love you!

Dad, Mom, and Nancy

COREY DEPOOTER

Age: 17
Junior

Corey was a young man who was full of life. He was a person that you would want to spend time with. He loved to talk and could have long conversations on the subjects he was passionate about. With his sense of humor Corey could have a whole room laughing.

Corey was an outdoorsman at heart. Every free hour he had he spent fishing. He loved the mountains, camping with his family, hunting, golfing, and fly fishing at Yellowstone.

Corey had just turned seventeen and was excited about his future. He was working at a golf course to save up for his first car. His goal was to become an officer in the Marine Corps. Corey looked forward to becoming a husband and a father and sharing his faith with his children.

Corey cherished his family, his friends, and his life.

KELLY FLEMING

Age: 16
Sophomore

A writer and a poet, a gentle soul who walked among us.

CAN THAT BE

I step outside, what did I hear?
I heard the whispers,
And the cries of the people's fear.
The loneliness of wisdom,
Can that be?
The sad, sad, sorrow that I see,
That is past in the trees,
Is it true, can it be real?
Can I let them know how I really feel?
The things that I have seen,
The things that I have felt,
The feelings of sorrow
That I hope I will soon melt.
Wherever I looked,
Wherever I turned,
I see shadows all through the night.
I put my head down and said a little prayer,
To tell the Lord the sad, sad, sorrow,
And the lonely cries that I have heard.
After a minute of silence, of wisdom,
I looked up slowly,
I saw a thing that I have never seen.
I saw a light and asked myself can that be?
Was it real or was it a dream?
I didn't know but hopefully

It will come to me.
It was bright and I was scared.
I didn't know what or if I should see.
I looked and then it came to me.
It was a dream.
When I was turning to walk away,
I heard a voice.

Written by Kelly in 1998. Her first draft; final draft published in *Chicken Soup for the Teenage Soul III.*

MATTHEW KECHTER

Age: 16

Sophomore

Matthew, a gift from God.

As the sun rises, the eagle soars, and the wind whispers, we will remember you. Memories are moments of time strung together, but in these moments of reflection we will see the kindness in your eyes, hear your sweet chuckles of laughter, and feel the love for others in your heart. We will always remember your fondness for the outdoors, your passion for sports and your dedication to academic success. Your broad and proud grin after you caught your first trout will never be forgotten. You loved to compete and strive for the best in all sports that you played. You loved to win, yet your sense of fairness and integrity always prevailed. Academically you shined so very bright. Never forgotten will be the moment when you were listening to music, watching a football game and working on your Algebra. When questioned about the distractions, using your Forrest Gump voice you replied, "I have a 4.0, and that is all I am going to say about that." Known as the go-to guy for homework help, you always found time to lend a hand. More importantly, you brought joy to those around you with a kind word or a gentle smile. Your devotion to family and friends will serve as your inspiration to follow as we journey through life. You possessed such profound empathy for someone so young. You were so wise, loving and thoughtful.

"I am with you always." Matthew 28:20

DANIEL MAUSER

Age: 15
Sophomore

It is not easy to sum up the life of a son and brother. To his parents, he was a first-born gift with spiritual dimensions that caused us to seek a deeper life. To his sister Christine, he was a fun companion but also one who was willing to share his wisdom and knowledge. To his sister Madeline he will be the brother who was never known, but whose presence will always be felt. To others he will be an inspiration for how he tackled his own weaknesses and often overcame them in surprising ways.

We remember Daniel as a boy with a gentle spirit and a shy grin. Often charming and sometimes intense, he was just coming into his own. He still saw the world through largely innocent eyes. He was an inquisitive and occasionally maddening adolescent who would challenge you to examine your assumptions about most everything.

In the most profound sense, however, Daniel was one who, despite difficulties, knew the ineffable sweetness of life and it was part of him. It was our great blessing to have had him as a member of our family.

DANIEL ROHRBOUGH

Age: 15
Freshman

March 2, 1984-April 20, 1999
What will the world miss?

(Left half)

A precious gift from God with an engaging smile and beautiful blue eyes that would light up the room, sensitive and caring, always quick with a comforting hug. A funny kid with an infectious laugh and a quick-come-back, so full of questions and wanting to know how things worked. Family was important to you and always included in your life. Just beginning your journey with so much to learn, yet you taught us so much. We miss you...

(Right half)

"Dad, I have a question." Why? My son, in a Nation that legalized the killing of innocent children in the womb; in a Country where authorities would lie and cover up what they knew and what they did; in a Godless school system your life was taken...Dan, I'm sorry. *"I love you dad, I'll see you tomorrow."*

7:00 p.m. April 19, 1999.

"There is no peace," says the Lord, *"for the wicked."* Isaiah 48:22

WILLIAM "DAVE" SANDERS

Age: 47
Teacher/coach

Born in Illinois, as a child he liked Davey Crockett, little league baseball and loved the sound of a bouncing basketball. Dave's young life was mentored by his high school basketball coach. He played basketball and ran cross-country in college then began his career as a business teacher and coach. Dave encouraged students, family members and friends to become better people through kindness and encouragement. He inspired many people to achieve their dreams and his spirit lives on in everyone who loved him or knew him. Know that he loves you all and is with you always.

He will always be only one thought away when we need strength and comfort. We have a lifetime filled with memories of a man we are so proud to have known. So, remember Dave for how he lived; not how he died.

We are grateful for his final words: "Tell my girls I love them", we love you too.

RACHEL SCOTT

Age: 17
Junior

Her middle name described her; she was a Joy! Her beauty reflected her kindness and compassion. A month before her death she wrote: "*I have this theory that if one person can go out of their way to show compassion, then it will start a chain reaction of the same. People will never know how far a little kindness can go.*"

Rachel had a sense of destiny and purpose. She also had a premonition her life would be short. She wrote: "*Just passing by, just coming through, not staying long. I always knew this home I have will never last.*" The day she died, she told a teacher: "*I'm going to have an impact on the world.*"

In her diary, she wrote: "*I won't be labeled as average.*"

Her faith in God was expressed in a prayer she wrote: "*I want to serve you; I want to be used by you to help others.*" Her final words were testimony to her life. When asked if she believed in God, she replied, "*You know I do!*"

ISAIAH SHOELS

Age: 18
Senior

The love of God was first in Isaiah's life. The love for his parents, Vonda and Michael, was the highlight of his life. His close relationship with his grandmother Bessie showed in his respect for others. He loved sports, playing and joking with his family, and was taught to love others no matter how they treated him. Isaiah died in a room filled with hate and darkness. He now lives in a beautiful room filled with heavenly light and beauty. He would want you to look up and see the light, to put away the guns, hate, prejudice, and pride, and see the great light that is love. He is one of the beautiful flowers God has picked for his heavenly Garden, to shine and to be an everlasting light

Isaiah, we will always miss you. We will always love you. With love from your Family and friends.

Stop doing wrong, learn to do right. Isaiah 1:15-17

Maintain justice and do what is right. Isaiah 56: 1-2

Those who walk uprightly enter into peace. Isaiah 57: 1-2

JOHN TOMLIN

Age: 16
Sophomore

Born September 1, John Tomlin was a young man with a broad smile and bright eyes. As a kid he loved cars, baseball, family and God. As a teen he added Chevy trucks and the Green Bay Packers to that list, and his love for Jesus developed in him a strong set of Christian morals.

John had a gentle disposition that parents and girlfriends dream of; the kind that didn't need a heavy hand of discipline and that made him an old-fashioned gentleman on dates. But his sunny disposition could not keep him from entering what many teens enter; a dark tunnel of loneliness where God seemed far away.

John didn't stay long in that tunnel. Seven months before his death he reconnected with God and rediscovered the joy of his faith. That faith sustained John with courage and strength to face evil during the last moments of his life in the Columbine High School library. In heaven now, John fully understands the truth of the words written long ago: *"You, dear children, are from God and have overcome them, because the one who is in you is greater than the one who is in the world."* 1 John 4:4

LAUREN TOWNSEND

Age: 18
Senior

Excerpts from Lauren's Diary

A woman in the middle of a field of flowers kissing Jesus' wounds; I didn't think I could draw such a beautiful picture. I did tonight. It took me only two hours. I think something was guiding me other than just my hand. That is my dream. When I die, I want to wake up in a field of flowers and see Jesus sitting there smiling, happy to see me, holding my hand. Then I want to kiss his wounds. Maybe it sounds corny, but I can't even describe how happy I would be if I could do that. Then I would hug him, he'd kiss me on the forehead and we would just sit there hugging in the sun with the wind blowing in our hair. The wind is God because God is everywhere. Just that moment is worth living many lives for.

I feel so peaceful, calm and joyful; like I am on the verge of enlightenment. There is so much more going on here than we realize. I do think humanity is losing touch with itself and their relationship with their surroundings. Unfortunately it usually takes a huge trauma to get people to realize what is important and I feel that is what is going to happen to wake up everyone to get in touch with their spiritual sides. I am not afraid of death for it is only a transition. For, in the end all there is, is love.

KYLE VELASQUEZ

Age: 16
Sophomore

A young man, who as a child struggled with developmental delays and learning disabilities. He knew his limitations, yet wanted to be like every other kid. He was just beginning to really like who he was. Kyle taught those who loved him so much about unconditional love, compassion, forgiveness, perseverance, and acceptance. He was a true friend to those who chose to take the time to know him. He loved his brother Daniel, the family cats, ice cream, pizza, and riding his bike. He spent his time at home with his family, watching sports with dad and going to the library with mom. Kyle had been a student at Columbine only three months and was just beginning to spread his wings. The world around him was beginning to open up for a young boy who had struggled through school and life. But, through all his delays and difficulties he always smiled, forgave and saw the GOOD in those around him.

Kyle was and is very much loved. He will always be missed and never forgotten.

We will never forget them.

Acknowledgments

I have named many in the dedication and body of this book, and in most cases, I hope my gratitude is obvious. I know that even after repeating and adding names here, I will have left out someone who deserves my thanks.

Please accept my apologies in advance for that.

Once more, In Loving Memory of the Beloved Thirteen.
My heart goes out to their families—always—and
to the wounded and others affected.

Thanks to . . .

83rd Circle Families for their support and love of Diane and me

The DiPetro Family

The Marchese Family

The Rosson Family

Mount Carmel Classmates, Alumni, Staff Members

Ranum High School Classmates, Alumni, Staff Members

Metropolitan State College Fellow Students, Alumni, Staff Members

Jefferson County Schools Board Members

Jefferson County Schools District Administrators

Law Enforcement Agencies and First Responders

Local Hospitals

Craig Hospital   Kenny Hosack

Administrators Association (JCAA)

Mary McNeil

Jefferson County Education Association (JCEA)

Colorado Association of School Executive (CASE)

Bruce Caughey

Colorado High School Activities Association (CHSSA)

Bob Ottewill   Paul Angelico
Bill Reader

Colorado Baseball Dugout Club

Fellow educators and coaches

Caplan and Earnest Law Firm Team:

Susan Schermerhorn   Jim Branum
Bill Kowalski   Alex Halpern
Allen Taggart   Stu Stuller

National Association of School Resource Officers (NASRO):

Mo Canady   Seth Sullivan
Kerri Williamson   Ed Bova

Denver Athletics

Mick Montgomery   Bruce Beck

All the organizers of conferences for the opportunity to share my message and presenters with whom I have shared a stage:

Kristina Anderson
Stacy Avila
Dr. Tony Bates
Dr. David Benke
Kevin Cameron
Theresa Campbell
Mo Canady
AJ DeAndrea
Lisa Dinhofer
James Englert
Brian Gard
Michele Gay
Lt. Col. David Grossman
Pat Hamilton
Natalie Hammond
Lisa Hamp

CJ Huff
Dr. Bernie James
Sam Jingfors
Heather Martin
John McDonald
Dr. Carolyn Lunsford Mears
Brian Murphy
John Nicoletti
Carly Posey
Jackie Schildkraut
Jackie Sulfaro
Stan Szptek
Mark Thompson
Paul Timm
Diane Varano
Steve Wilder

You are making a difference!

Also to . . .

John Akers
Scott Bemis
Donnie Bruno
Harry Bull
Jerry Capoot
Ed Clarke
Dan Cohan
Steve Davis
The Findling Family
Gary Fuller
Ron Gabbert
Sam Granillo
Trevor Greene
Jim Jenkins
Rick Kaufman
Gina Kirkland
George Latuda

Pender Makins
Don Martin
Debbie Meaux
Jerry Middleton
Dave and Cathy Mumper
Frank Palmeri
Mark Pendleton
Dino Pignataro
MaryAnn Pratt
Marilyn Saltzman
Lynn Setzer
Dr. Roy Siegfried
Max Swanson
Betsy Thompson
Craig Whaley
Willie White

In Memory of my aunts and uncles who instilled the values that I have today:

Tony and Irma DeAngelis

Ernie and Betty DeAngelis

Vito and Florence DeAngelis

Bea DeAngelis Ferrera

Sam Ferrera

Alfonso and Francis DeAngelis

Mary DeAngelis VanGieson

Mike VanGieson

Mary Satriano Ligrani

Jerry Ligrani

Roxie and Violet Satriano

Joe and Rose Satriano

Nettie Satriano Scarpello

Frank Scapello

Louise Satriano Gavito

Gus Gavito

Sue Satriano Colonno

Rick Colonno

To My Extended Family Members for always being there for me:

Libby Stickles

Florence Cookie DeAngelis

Tony and Angel DeAngelis Librizzi

Tony and Mary Ann DeAngelis Durbano

Peter DeAngelis

Tommy DeAngelis

Danny and Nancy DeAngelis Gargaro

John and Veda DeAngelis Dowd

Michael and Mary Ferrera

Tommy and Barb Ferrera

Bobby and Diane Ferrera McLaughlin

Kenny and Diane DeAngelis

Ernie and Debbie VanGieson

Peter and Kay VanGieson

Robert and Betty Ligrani

Anthony and Shirley Ligrani

Don and Roxanne Ritchie

LeEllen Satriano

Joe and Geraldine Satriano Lee

Diane Scarpello Jennings

Jerry Jennings

JoAnn Satriano

Joey Satriano

June Satriano

Fran Gavito

Rich and Sherry Gavito

Jimmy and Carol Gavito

Kenny and Sheryl Gavito

Barbie Colonno

Ricky and Mary Colonno

To media professionals for their support of me and the members of the Columbine High School community:

Dave Aguilera
Adele Arakawa
Jim Benemann
Ernie Bjorklund
Anastasia Bolton
Shaun Boyd
Peter Boyles
Irv Brown
Dan Caplis
Kim Christiansen
Kyle Clark
Sandy Clough
Marty Coniglio
Katie Couric
Patty Dennis
Neil Devlin
Becky Ditchfield
Amelia Earhart
John Ferrugia
Nelson Garcia
Alan Gionet
Drew Goodman
Tom Green
Jeff Hamrick
Chris Hansen
Scott Hastings
Julie Hayden
Lester Holt
Molly Hughes
Mitch Jelniker
Kyle Kendrick
Dave Knida
Mark Koebrich
Mike Landis
Lee Larson

Vic Lombardi
Rod Mackey
Darren "DMac" McKee
Lois Melkonian
Greg Moody
Gregg Moss
Mike Nelson
Christine Noel
Barry Peterson
Kim Posey
Cheryl Preheim
Alex Ramirez
Joe Rico
Corey Rose
Kathy Sabine
Rick Sallinger
Ed Sardella
Jerry Schemmel
Gary Shapiro
Craig Silverman
Kevin Simpson
Harry Smith
Deborah Takahara
TaRhonda Thomas
Anne Trujillo
Steffan Tubbs
Kevin Vaughan
Kathy Walker
Kathy Walsh
Alfred "Big Al" Williams
Joe Williams
Mark Wolfe
Ron Zappolo
April Zesbaugh

I'd also like to offer my sincere thanks to Terry Frei for helping me tell this story.

More from
DAVE BURGESS
Consulting, Inc.

Since 2012, DBCI has been publishing books that inspire and equip educators to be their best. For more information on our DBCI titles or to purchase bulk orders for your school, district, or book study, visit **DaveBurgessConsulting.com/DBCBooks**.

More from the Like a PIRATE Series

Teach Like a PIRATE by Dave Burgess

Explore Like a Pirate by Michael Matera

Learn Like a Pirate by Paul Solarz

Play Like a Pirate by Quinn Rollins

Run Like a Pirate by Adam Welcome

Lead Like a PIRATE Series

Lead Like a PIRATE by Shelley Burgess and Beth Houf

Balance Like a Pirate by Jessica Cabeen, Jessica Johnson, and Sarah Johnson

Lead with Culture by Jay Billy

Lead with Literacy by Mandy Ellis

Leadership & School Culture

Culturize by Jimmy Casas

Escaping the School Leader's Dunk Tank by Rebecca Coda and Rick Jetter

The Innovator's Mindset by George Couros

Kids Deserve It! by Todd Nesloney and Adam Welcome

Let Them Speak by Rebecca Coda and Rick Jetter

The Limitless School by Abe Hege and Adam Dovico

The Pepper Effect by Sean Gaillard

The Principled Principal by Jeffrey Zoul and
  Anthony McConnell

The Secret Solution by Todd Whitaker, Sam Miller, and
  Ryan Donlan

Start. Right. Now. by Todd Whitaker, Jeffrey Zoul, and
  Jimmy Casas

Stop. Right. Now. by Jimmy Casas and Jeffrey Zoul

Unmapped Potential by Julie Hasson and Missy Lennard

Your School Rocks by Ryan McLane and Eric Lowe

Technology & Tools

50 Things You Can Do with Google Classroom by Alice Keeler
  and Libbi Miller

50 Things to Go Further with Google Classroom by Alice Keeler
  and Libbi Miller

140 Twitter Tips for Educators by Brad Currie, Billy Krakower,
  and Scott Rocco

Code Breaker by Brian Aspinall

Creatively Productive by Lisa Johnson

Google Apps for Littles by Christine Pinto and Alice Keeler

Master the Media by Julie Smith

Shake Up Learning by Kasey Bell

Social LEADia by Jennifer Casa-Todd

Teaching Math with Google Apps by Alice Keeler and
  Diana Herrington

Teaching Methods & Materials

All 4s and 5s by Andrew Sharos

Ditch That Homework by Matt Miller and Alice Keeler

Ditch That Textbook by Matt Miller

Educated by Design by Michael Cohen

The EduProtocol Field Guide by Marlena Hebern and
 Jon Corippo

Instant Relevance by Denis Sheeran

LAUNCH by John Spencer and A.J. Juliani

Make Learning MAGICAL by Tisha Richmond

Pure Genius by Don Wettrick

Shift This! by Joy Kirr

Spark Learning by Ramsey Musallam

Sparks in the Dark by Travis Crowder and Todd Nesloney

Table Talk Math by John Stevens

The Classroom Chef by John Stevens and Matt Vaudrey

The Wild Card by Hope and Wade King

The Writing on the Classroom Wall by Steve Wyborney

Inspiration, Professional Growth, & Personal Development

The Four O'Clock Faculty by Rich Czyz

Be REAL by Tara Martin

Be the One for Kids by Ryan Sheehy

The EduNinja Mindset by Jennifer Burdis

How Much Water Do We Have? by Pete and Kris Nunweiler

P Is for Pirate by Dave and Shelley Burgess

The Path to Serendipity by Allyson Aspey

Sanctuaries by Dan Tricarico

Shattering the Perfect Teacher Myth by Aaron Hogan

Stories from Webb by Todd Nesloney

Talk to Me by Kim Bearden

The Zen Teacher by Dan Tricarico

Children's Books

Dolphins in Trees by Aaron Polansky

The Princes of Serendip by Allyson Apsey

Frank DeAngelis

Former Principal of Columbine High School

About the Author

Colorado-native **Frank DeAngelis** retired from his position as principal of Columbine High School after thirty-five years of service. He began his career there as social studies teacher and filled the roles of head baseball coach, assistant football coach, dean of students, and assistant principal, before becoming the principal in 1996.

After the tragic shootings on April 20, 1999, DeAngelis mourned with the Columbine community. He vowed to never forget those who were murdered, those who were injured, and all who were impacted by the tragedy. He dedicated his life and career to helping his students—his kids—recover. He committed to staying on as principal to help the students and the community heal. Columbine was his family.

In the years that followed the shootings, DeAngelis was named the Colorado High School Principal of the year and was one of three finalists for the National Principal of the Year. He has also received the Jefferson County Lifetime Achievement Award and the Gandhi, King, Ikeda Community Builders Award.

DeAngelis is often asked to speak and consult with schools and communities as they recover from acts of mass violence. He currently serves as a consultant for safety and emergency management for the Jeffco School District in Colorado and continues to deliver speeches in the United States, Canada, and Europe.

Terry Frei's seven books have drawn praise from Pulitzer Prize winners and other prominent journalists, reviewers, former presidents, high-profile athletes, fellow authors, and the public. His novels are *Olympic Affair* and *The Witch's Season*; and his non-fiction works include *Horns, Hogs, and Nixon Coming* and *Third Down and a War to Go*, plus *'77: Denver, the Broncos, and a Coming of Age*. As a journalist, he has been voted the National Sports Media Association's state sports writer of the year seven times—four times in Colorado and three times in Oregon. At the University of Colorado, he has been vice chair of the History Department Advisory Board and chair of the International Affairs Studies Advisory Board. He is an affiliate professor at Metropolitan State University of Denver and writes for *The Greeley Tribune* and *Mile High Sports magazine*. His web site is TerryFrei.com

CPSIA information can be obtained
at www.ICGtesting.com
Printed in the USA
LVHW110317260319
611849LV00001B/1/P

9 781949 595062